EASY PIANO SONGS

FOR BEGINNERS
LEVEL 2

SIMPLE SHEET MUSIC OF FAMOUS FAVORITES
TO PLAY WITH BOTH HANDS

COLLECTED AND ARRANGED BY
ANGELA MARSHALL

Easy Piano Songs for Beginners Level 2

Simple Sheet Music of Famous Favorites to Play with Both Hands

ISBN: 978-1-960555-19-9

Published by Avanell Publishing Inc

www.avanellpublishing.com

How to Use This Book

This book is designed to help you play the piano with both hands.
Start at the beginning of the book and work to the end to build your skills!

this music is too challenging for you, Level 1 books in this series include
music for one hand with no harmony. Start there and then try this book again.

you have trouble with rhythm, notes, or knowing how a song should sound,
sten to the included recordings. Listening is one of the best ways for
musicians to learn.

Bonus Downloads

This book includes free digital content.
Visit **www.avanellpublishing.com** or scan the QR code below
to access your bonus materials,

- Fully orchestrated recordings of each song

- Printable reference charts to use while you play

4

Table of Contents

How to Read Piano Music

A B C D E F G

Piano keys are named after the letters of the alphabet, but they only go to G!

The piano has black and white keys.
The black keys are arranged in groups of 2 and 3.

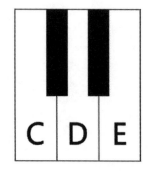

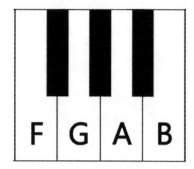

The letters **C D E**
are by a group of 2.

The letters **F G A B**
are by a group of 3.

The pattern of 2 and 3 repeats across the keyboard.
Use the groups of black keys to find the right notes on the piano.

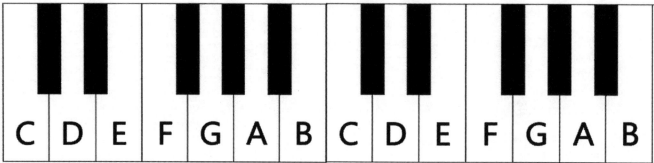

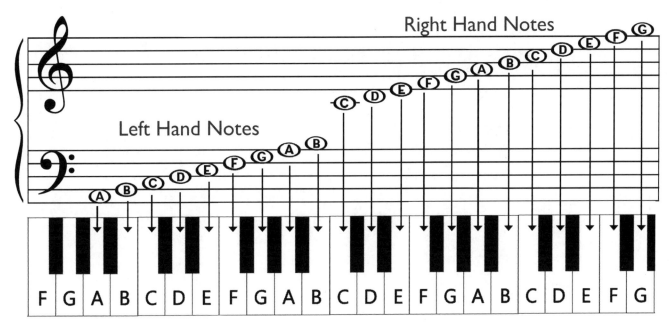

Each note is a letter of the musical alphabet and a key on the piano.

Each finger has a number.
Thumbs are number one!

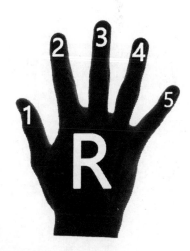

Each type of note gets a different number of beats.

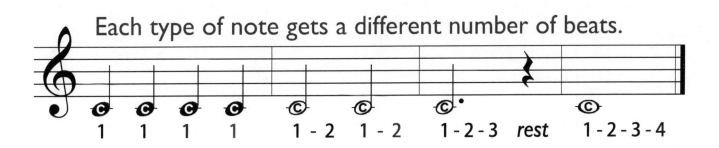

1   1   1   1   1 - 2   1 - 2   1 - 2 - 3   *rest*   1 - 2 - 3 - 4

Thumbs are Neighbors: Easy

All Songs in This Section Use Thumbs Are Neighbors Position

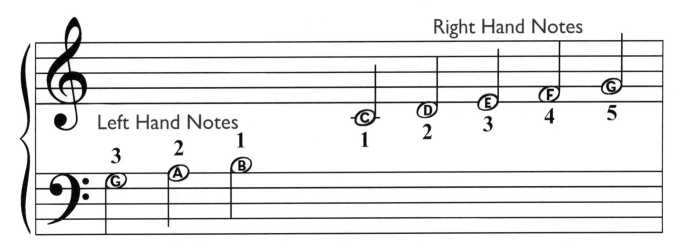

Notice that there are two G notes in this position.
One for left hand and one for right hand.

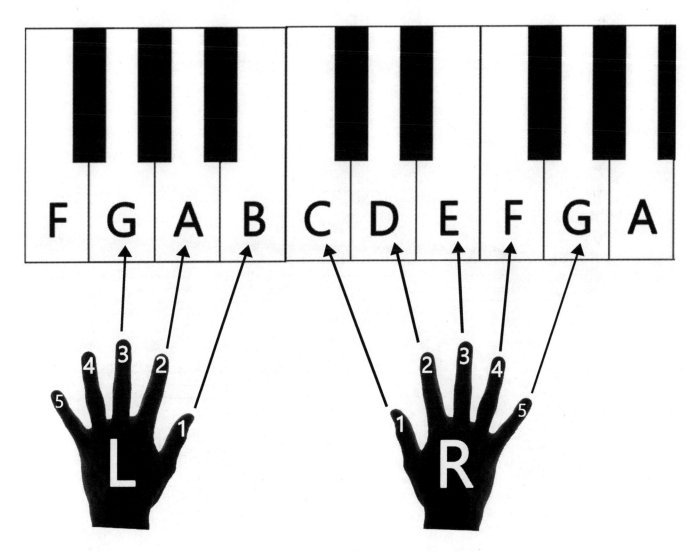

Thumbs Are Neighbors
Position Tutorial

Practice placing your hands in this position until you can do it quickly and easily.

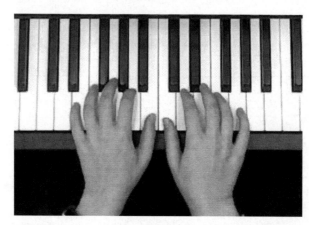

Every finger will sit on one note and play only that note.

Once your hands are in this position, don't move them.

Thumbs play on their sides.
All other fingers play on their fingertips.

Right hand notes
are written in the
treble clef.

Finger numbers
show you which
finger to use.

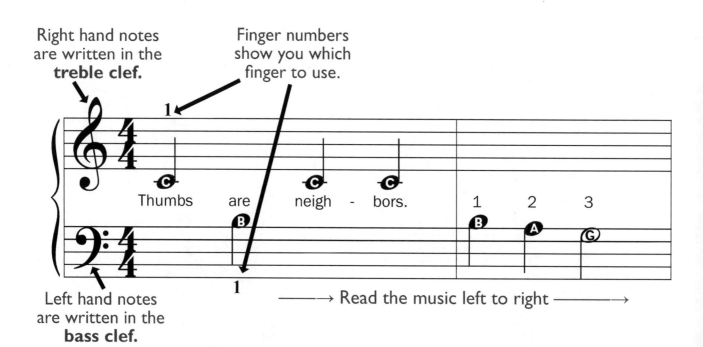

Thumbs are neigh - bors.

Read the music left to right

Left hand notes
are written in the
bass clef.

Thumbs Are Neighbors

Thumbs Are Neighbors Position

Angela Marshall

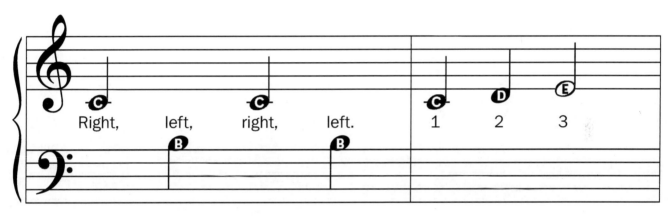

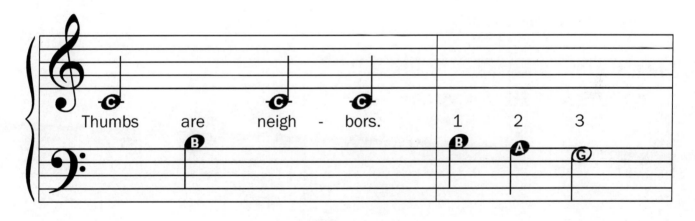

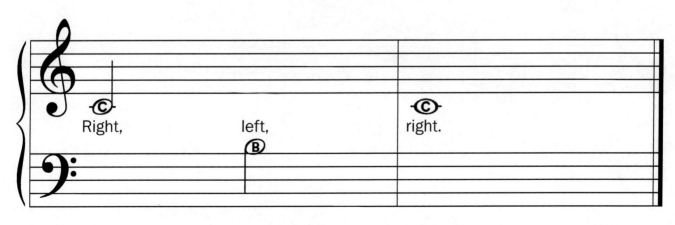

Twinkle, Twinkle, Little Star

Thumbs Are Neighbors Position

French Folk Tune with Lyrics by Jane Taylor

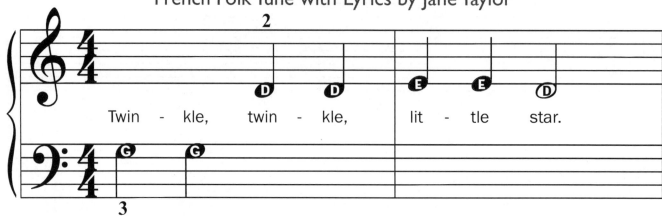

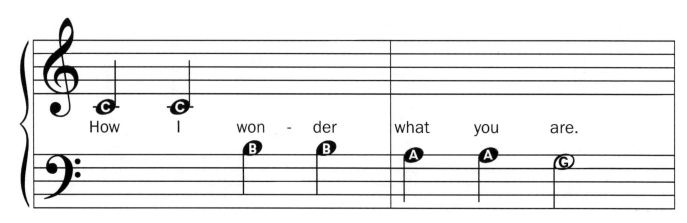

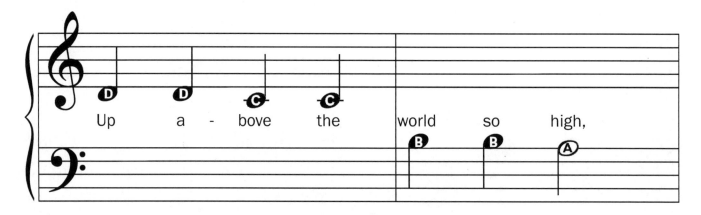

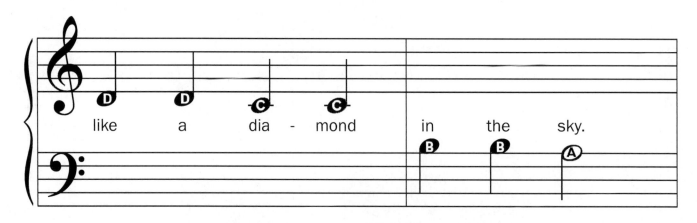

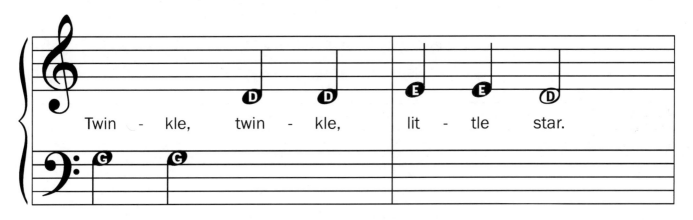

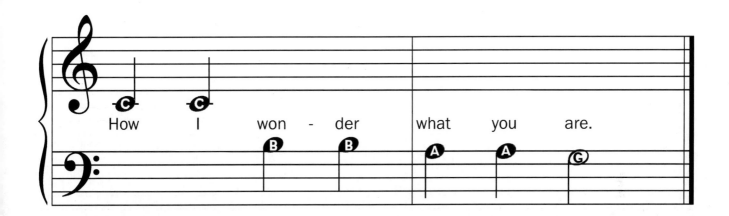

Old MacDonald Had a Farm

Thumbs Are Neighbors Position

Folk Song

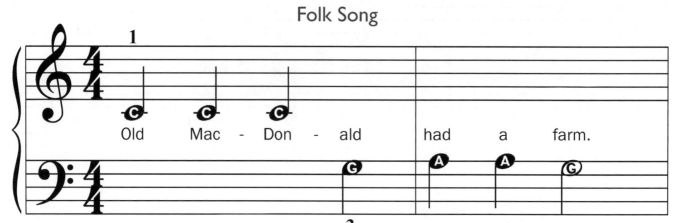

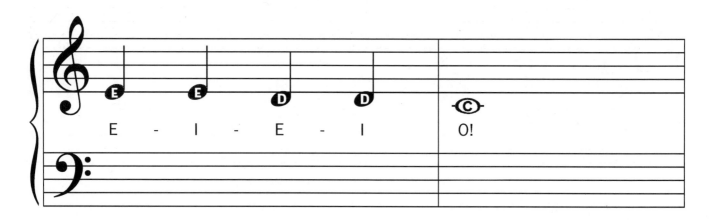

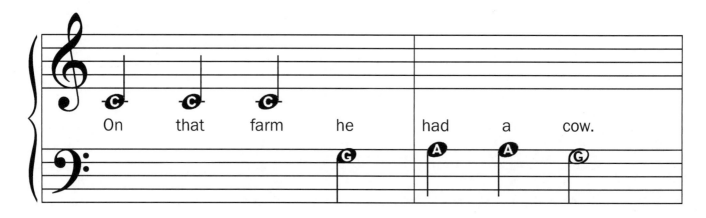

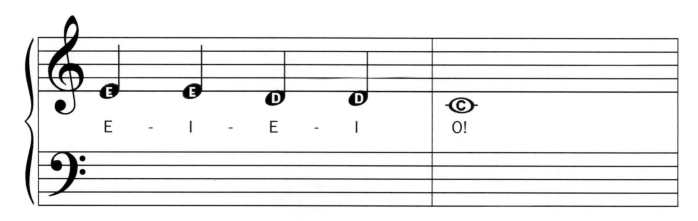

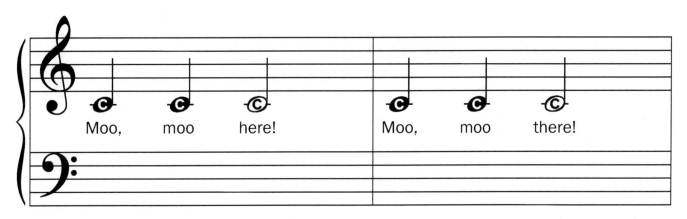

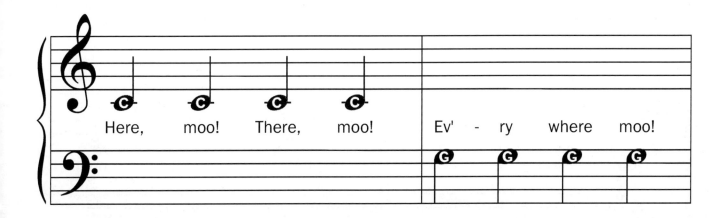

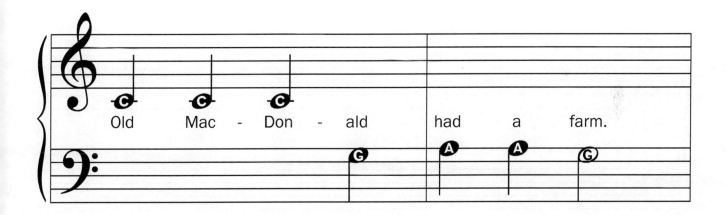

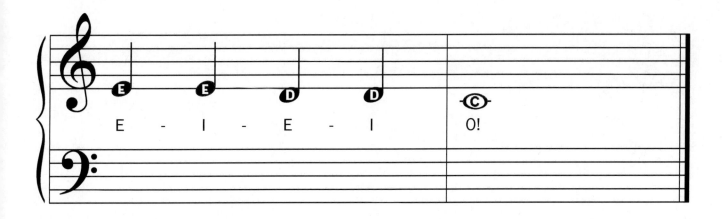

Baby Shark

Thumbs Are Neighbors Position
Traditional Campfire Chant

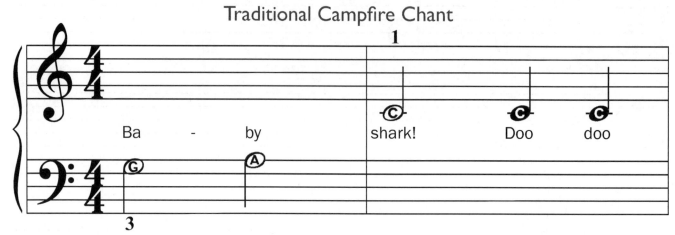

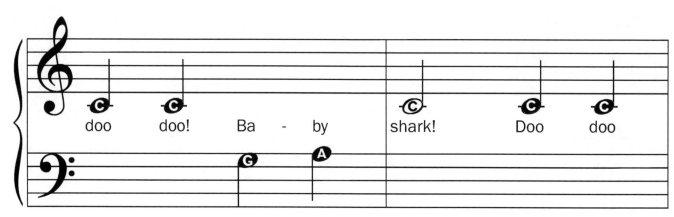

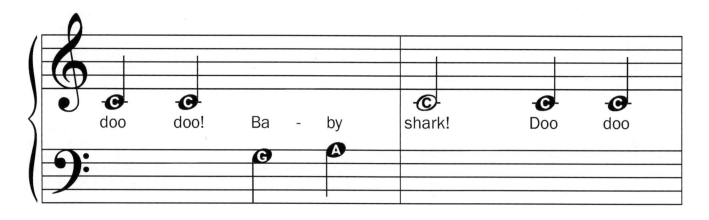

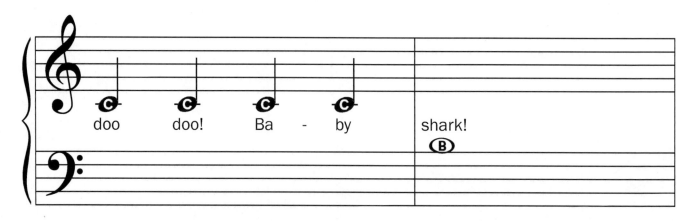

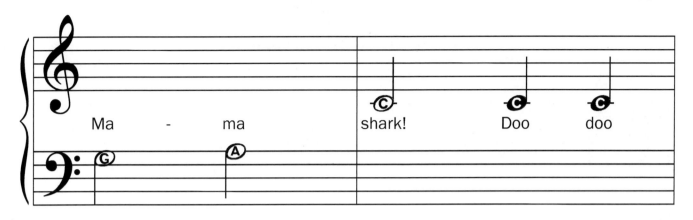

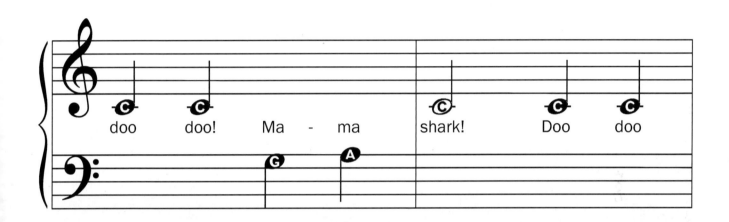

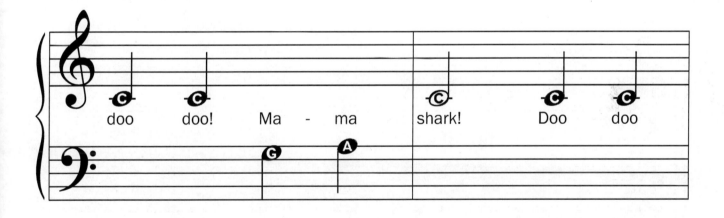

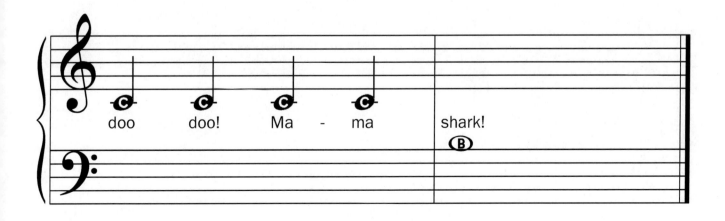

Rain, Rain, Go Away

Thumbs Are Neighbors Position

English Folk Song

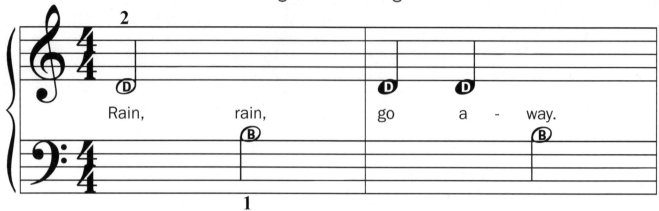

Rain, rain, go a - way.

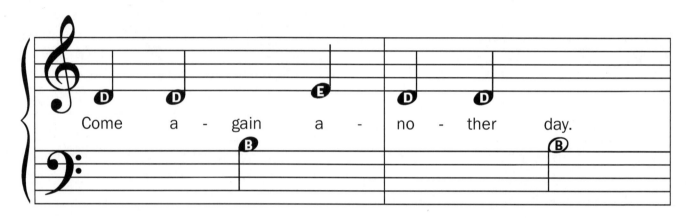

Come a - gain a - no - ther day.

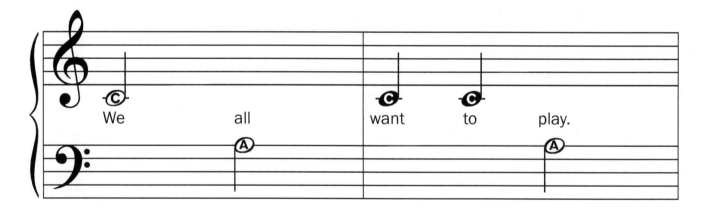

We all want to play.

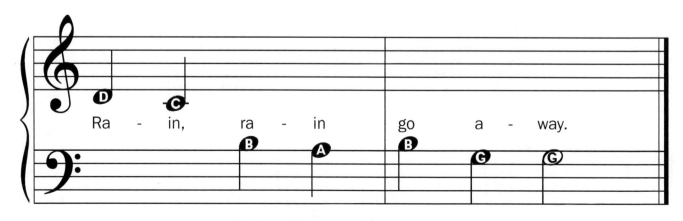

Ra - in, ra - in go a - way.

London Bridge is Falling Down

Thumbs Are Neighbors Position

English Folk Song

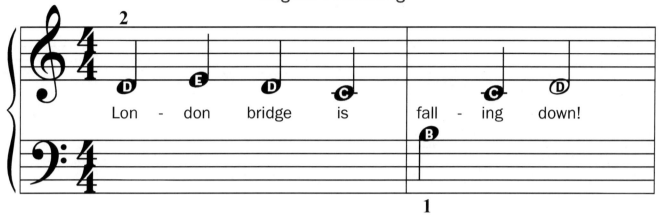

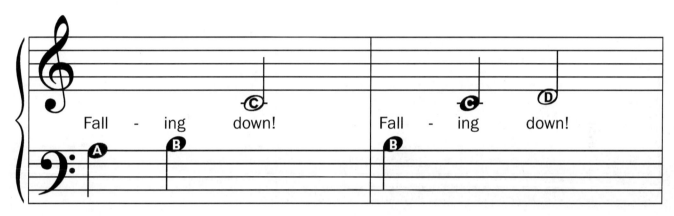

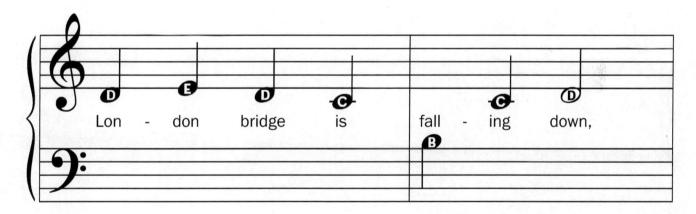

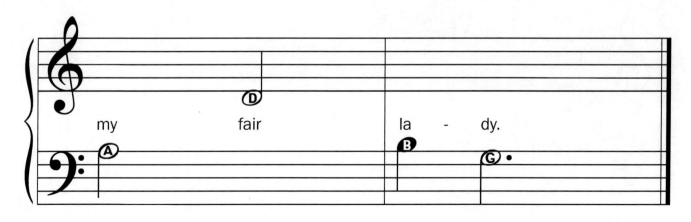

Bingo

Thumbs Are Neighbors Position

Traditional Folk Song

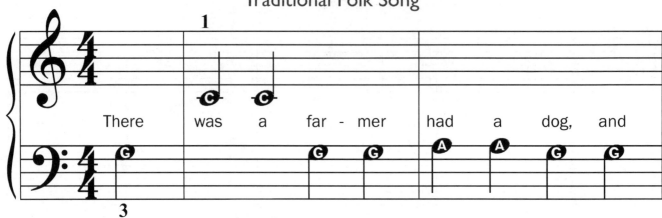

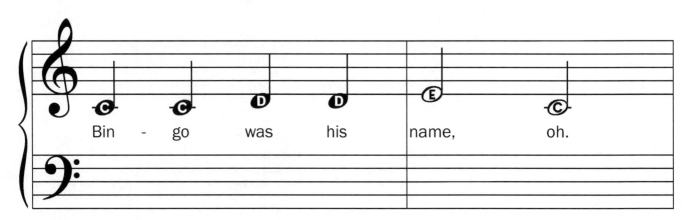

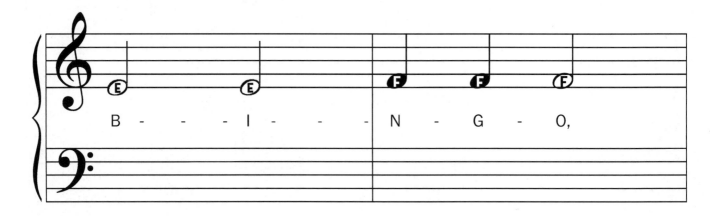

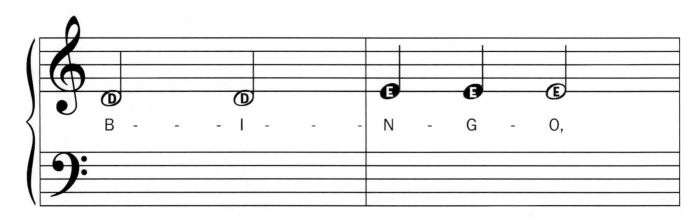

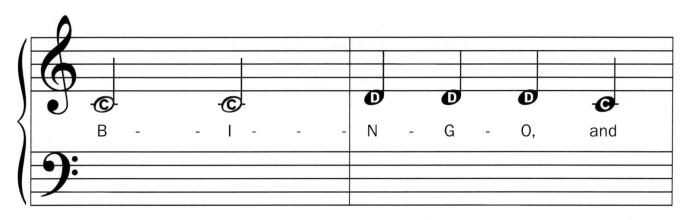

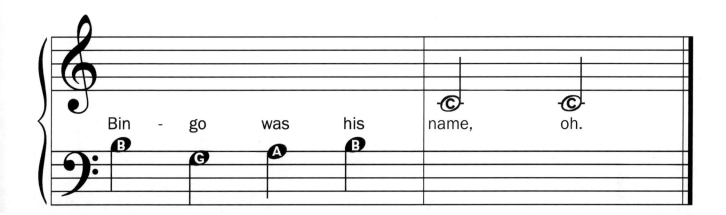

Yankee Doodle

Thumbs Are Neighbors Position

American Folk Song

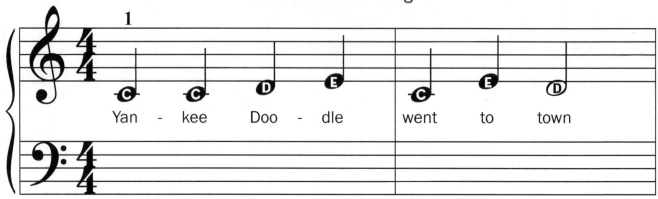

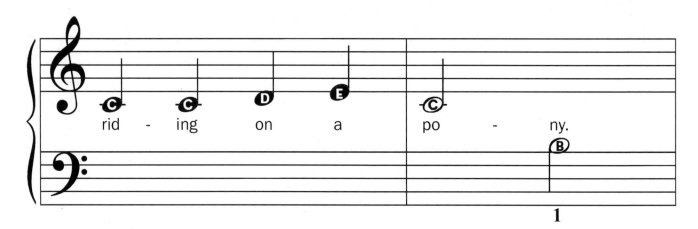

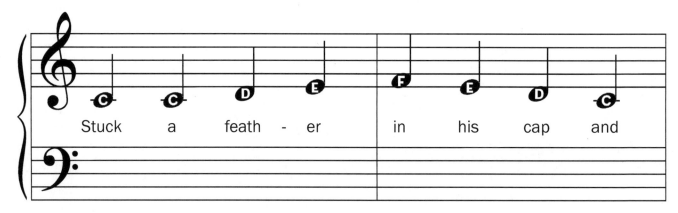

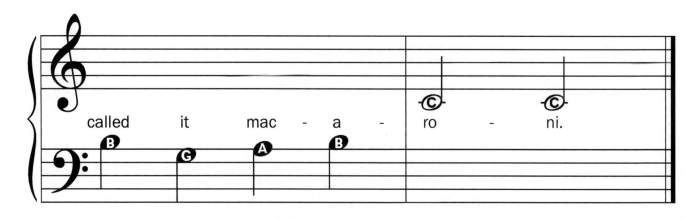

Surprise Symphony Theme

Thumbs Are Neighbors Position

Franz Joseph Haydn

The Muffin Man

Thumbs Are Neighbors Position

English Folk Song

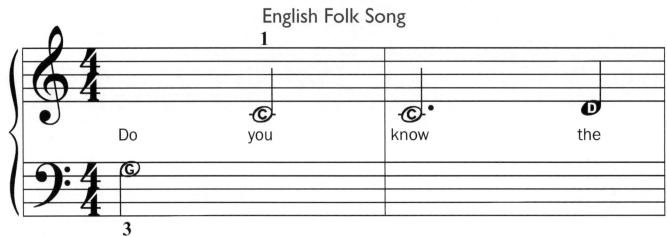

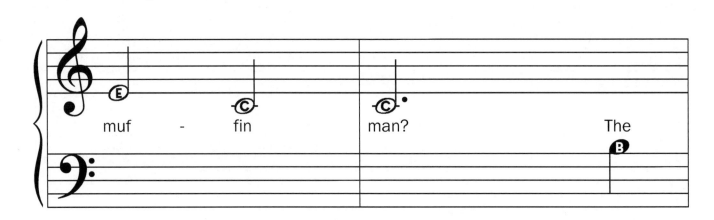

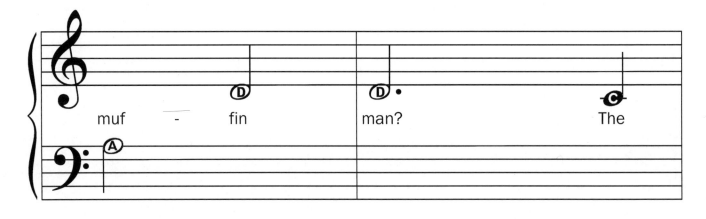

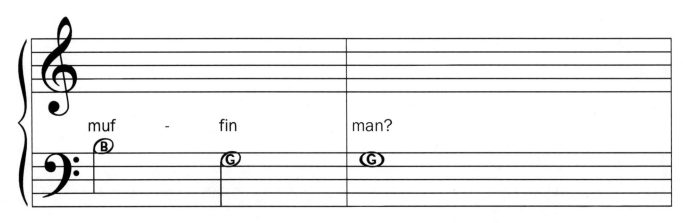

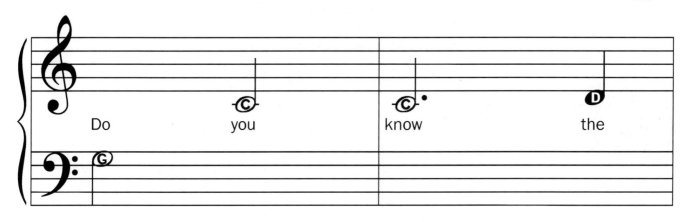

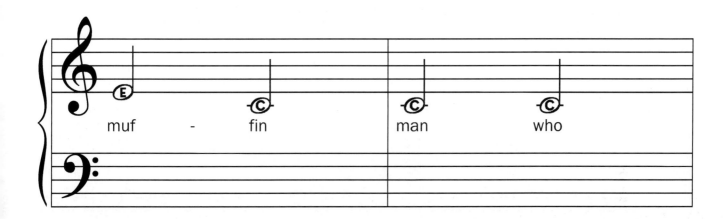

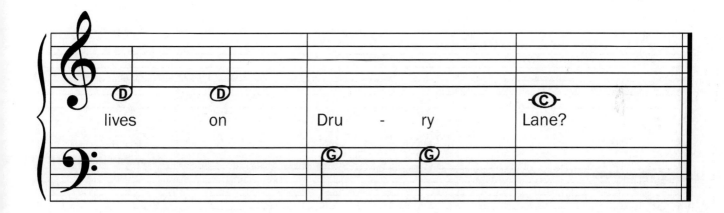

Halloween Waltz

Thumbs Are Neighbors Position
Angela Marshall

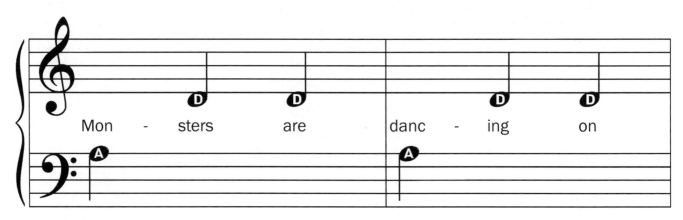

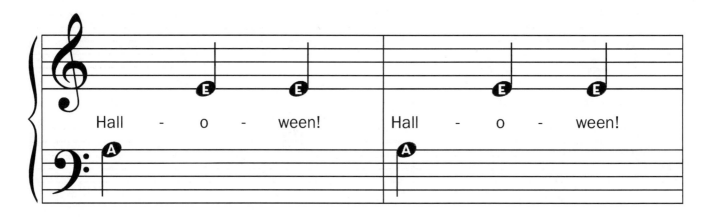

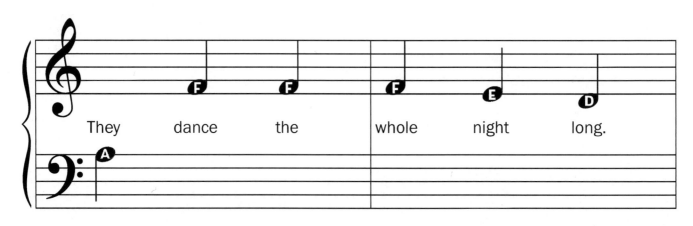

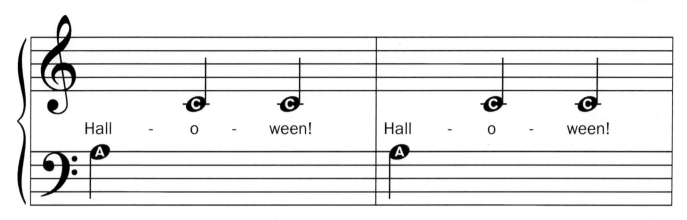

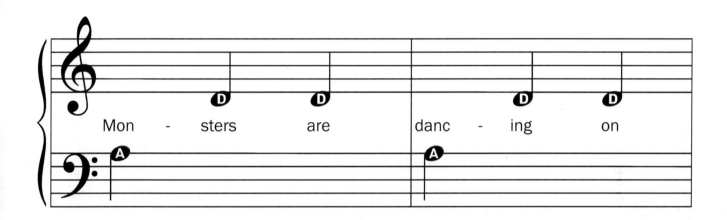

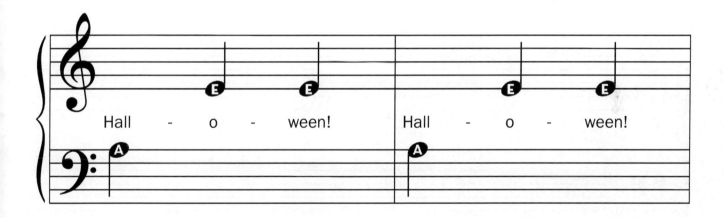

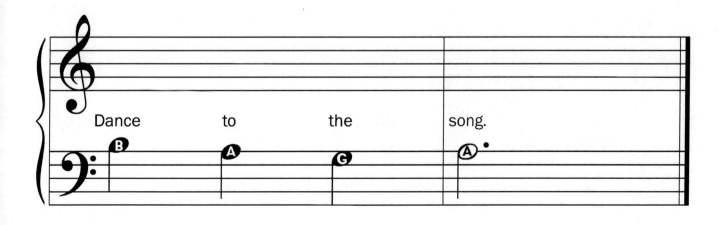

Hickory Dickory Dock

Thumbs Are Neighbors Position
English Nursery Rhyme

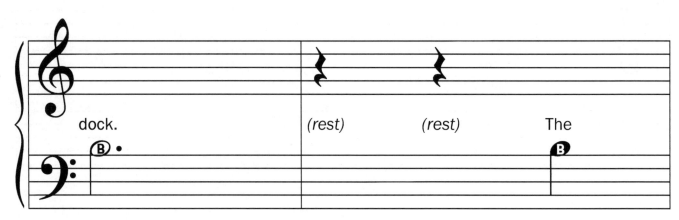

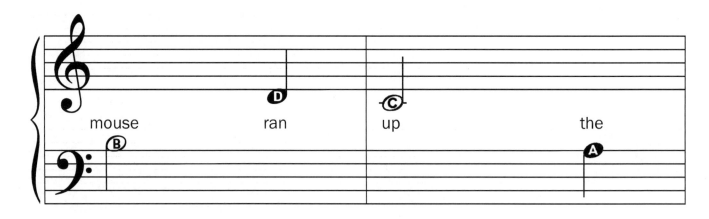

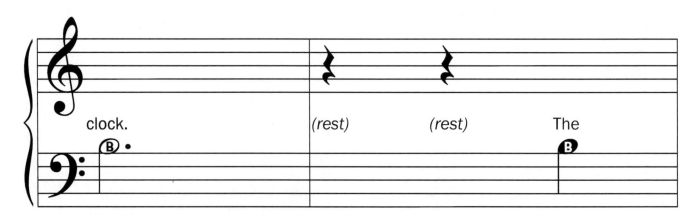

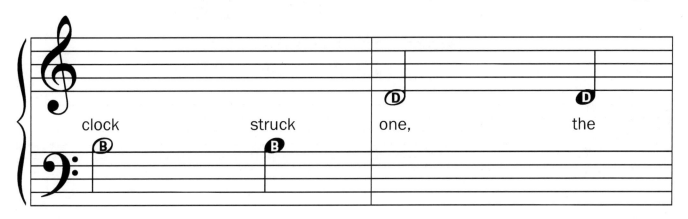

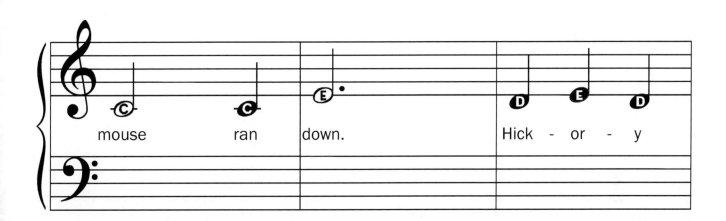

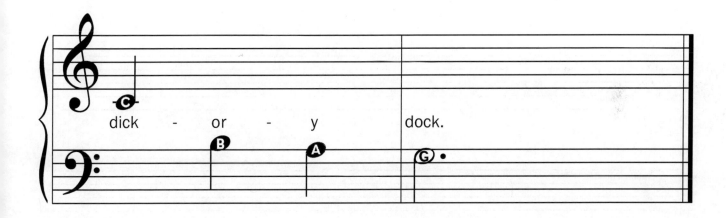

Cotton Eyed Joe

Thumbs Are Neighbors Position

American Folk Song

If it had - n't been for

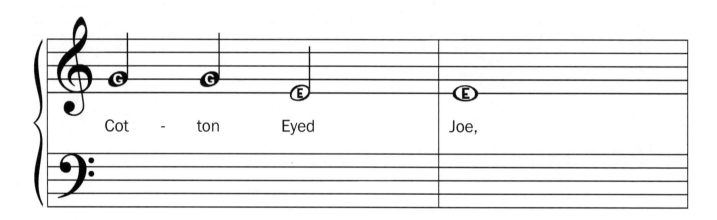

Cot - ton Eyed Joe,

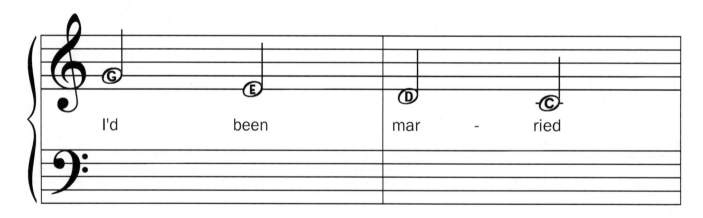

I'd been mar - ried

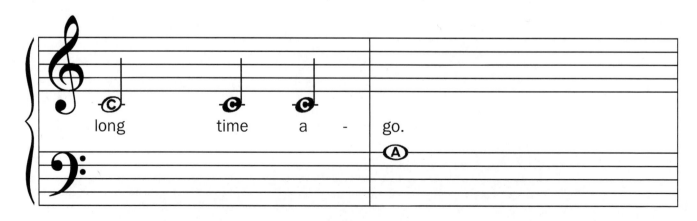

long time a - go.

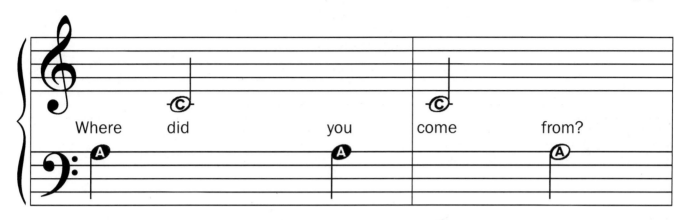

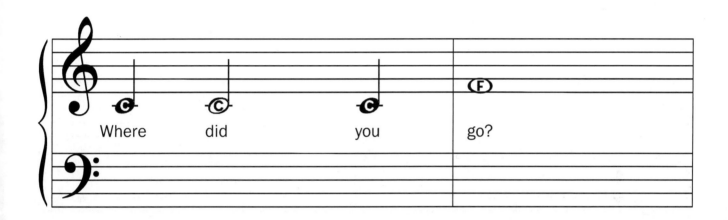

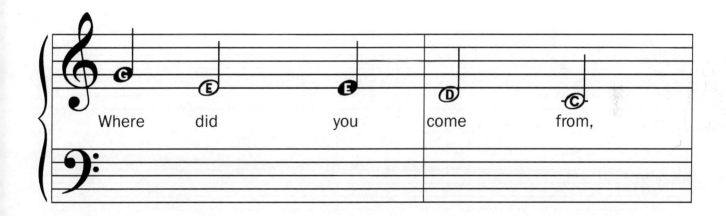

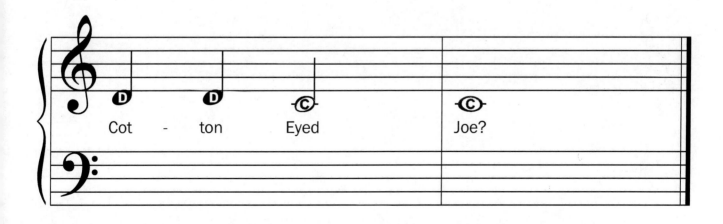

Bridal Chorus

Thumbs Are Neighbors Position

Richard Wagner

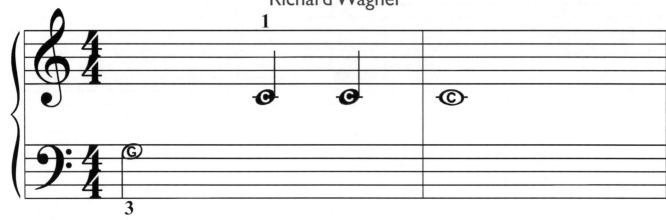

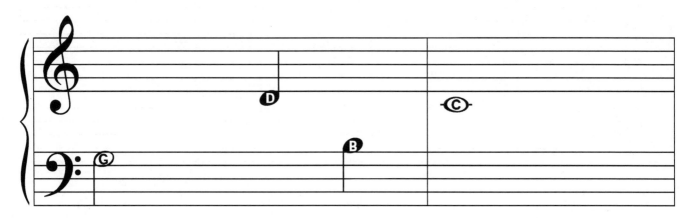

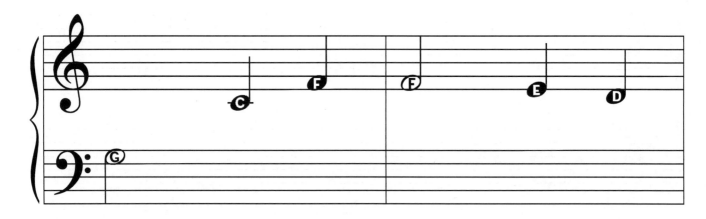

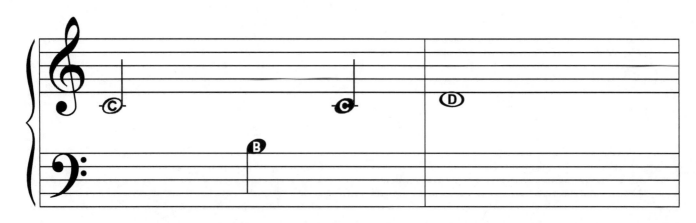

Scotland the Brave

Thumbs Are Neighbors Position
Scottish Folk Song

Thumbs Are Neighbors: Challenge

All Songs in This Section Use Thumbs Are Neighbors Position

But they include some challenges!

Some of these songs use sharps. **#**

Sharps tell you to play the black key directly to the right of the written note.

Move your fingers to the side to reach the sharps,
but keep the rest of your hand in position.

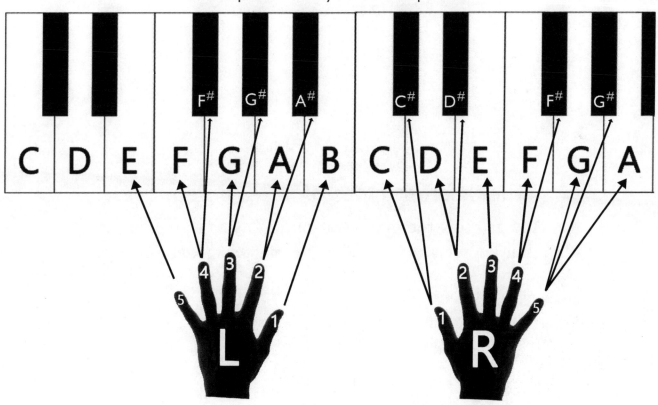

Move finger five to the
side to reach the note A.

Some Songs in This Section Use a New Type of Note

Notes connected by a flag get half a count each.
Two of them together equal a whole count.

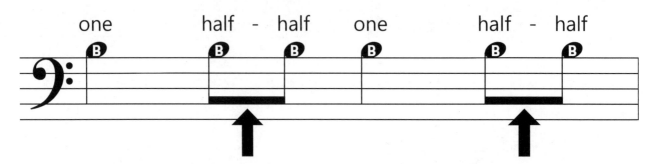

You can also count these notes by saying:
"Walk, run-ning, walk, run-ning."

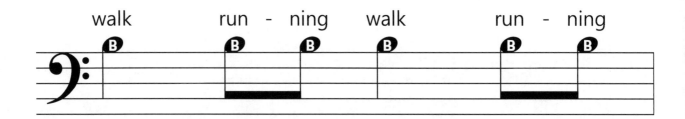

Note Names
The different types of notes have names.

You can play the piano without knowing the note names,
but knowing them makes it easier to talk about music.

Happy Birthday

Thumbs Are Neighbors Position

Patty and Mildred Hill

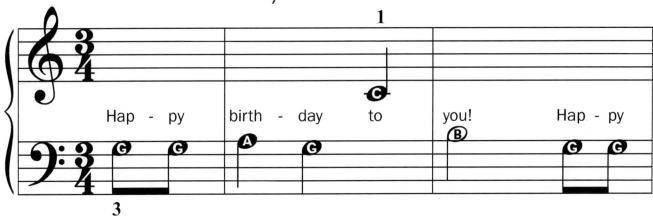

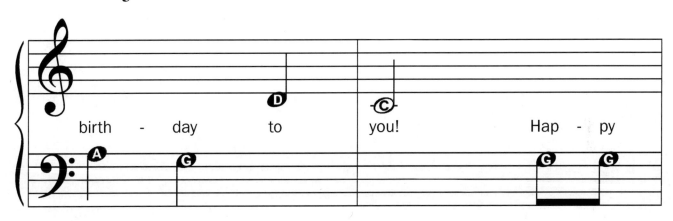

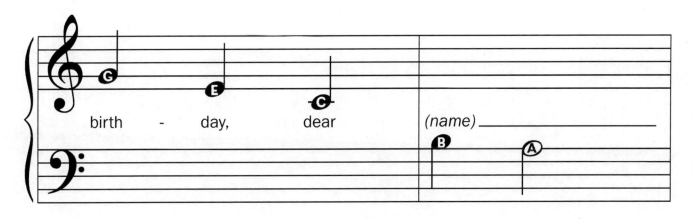

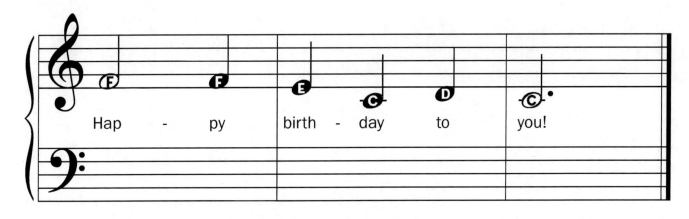

The Wheels on the Bus

Thumbs Are Neighbors Position

American Folk Song

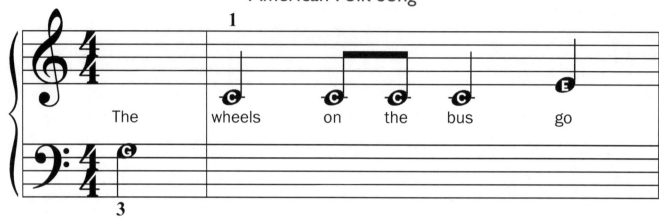

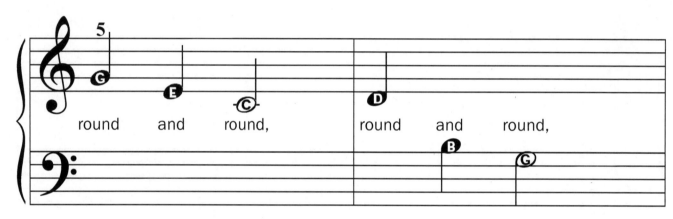

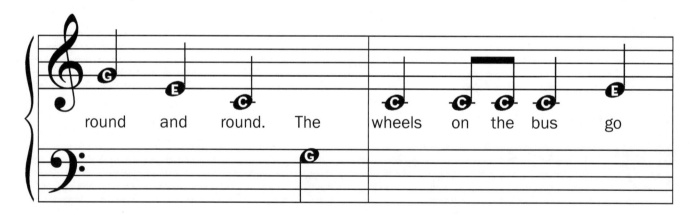

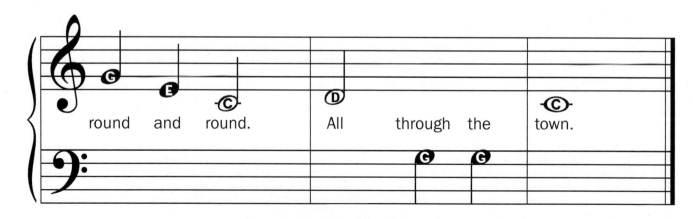

Oh Christmas Tree

Thumbs Are Neighbors Position

German Christmas Carol

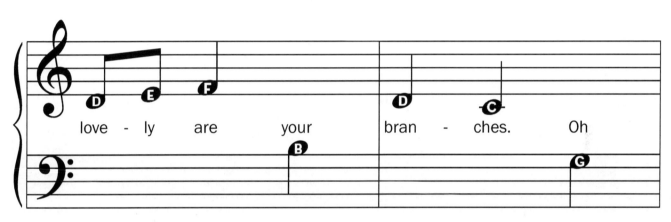

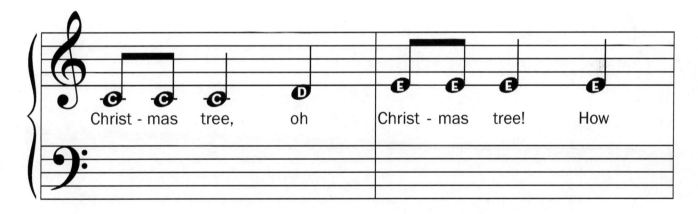

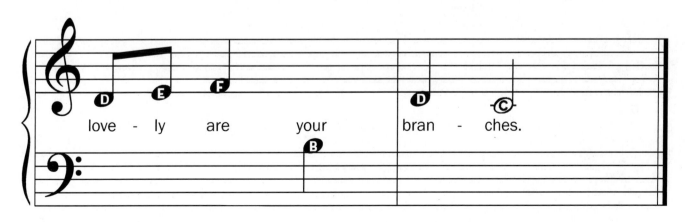

⁴² We Wish You a Merry Christmas

Thumbs Are Neighbors Position

English Christmas Carol

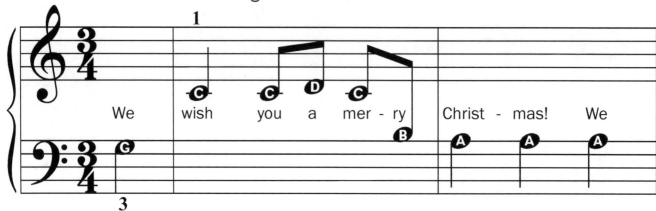

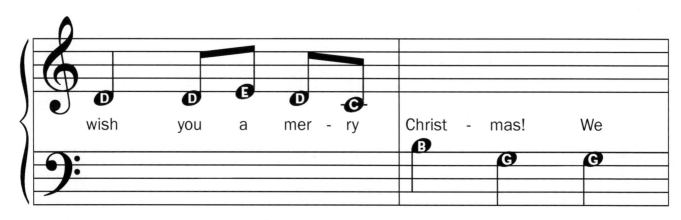

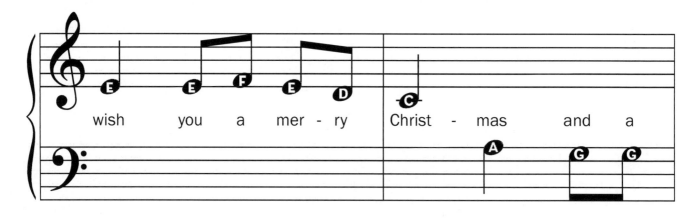

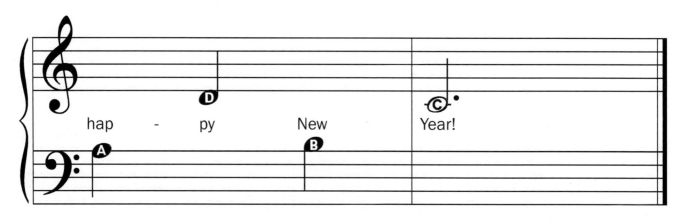

Up on the Housetop

Thumbs are Neighbors Position

Benjamin Hanby

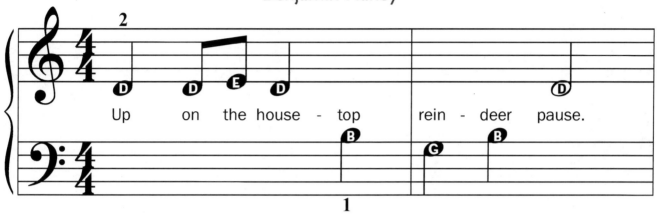

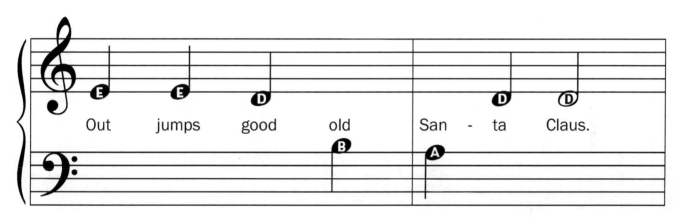

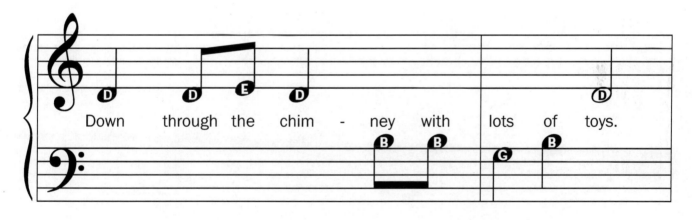

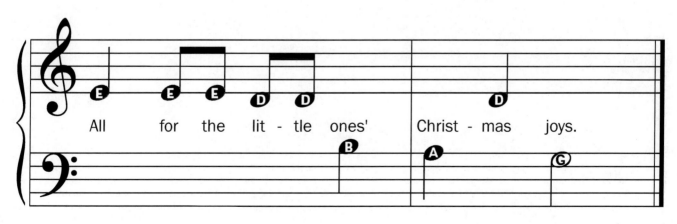

Home on the Range

Thumbs Are Neighbors Position

Dr. Brewster Higley and Daniel Kelley

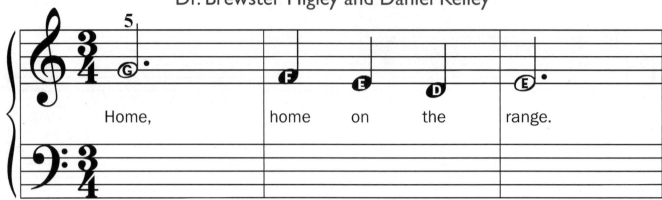

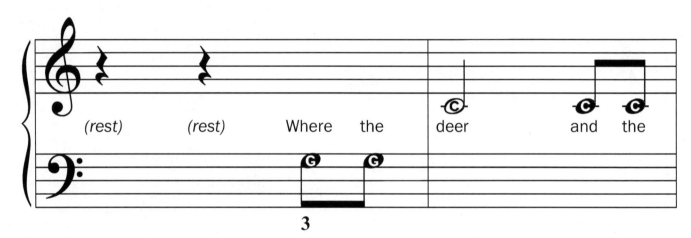

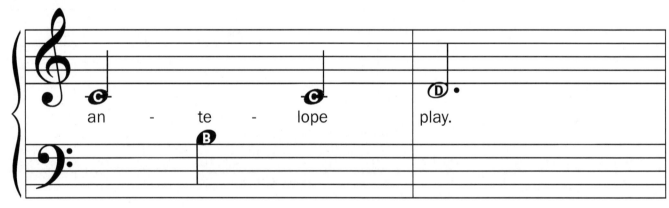

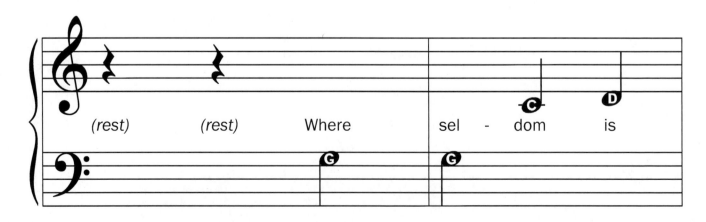

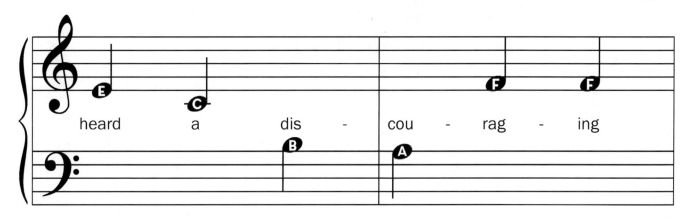

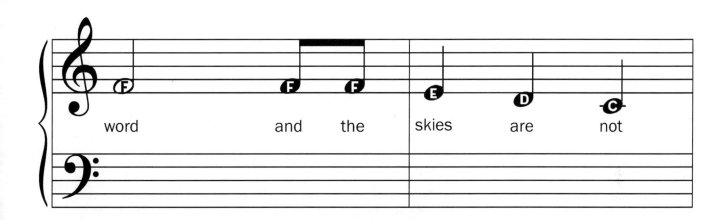

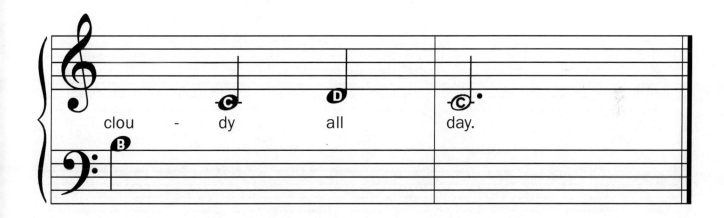

Amazing Grace

Thumbs Are Neighbors Position

John Newton and E. O. Excell

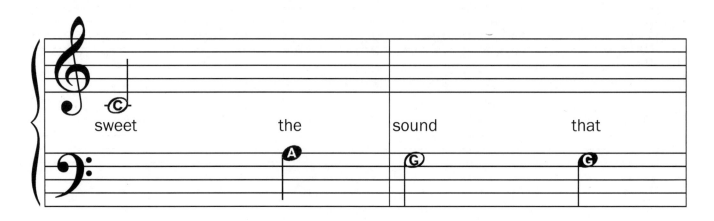

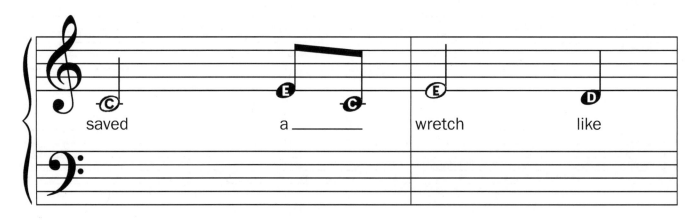

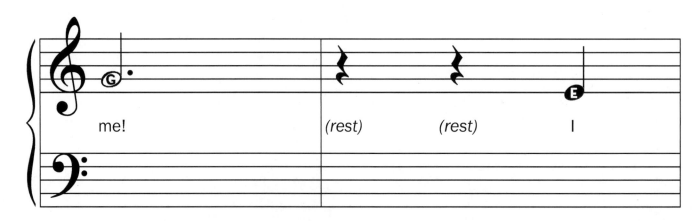

47

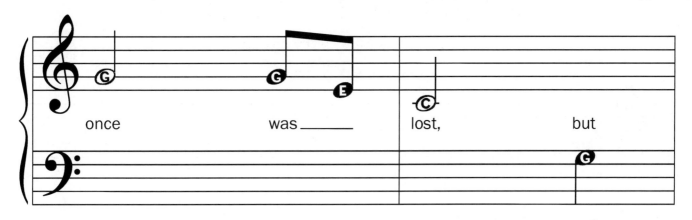

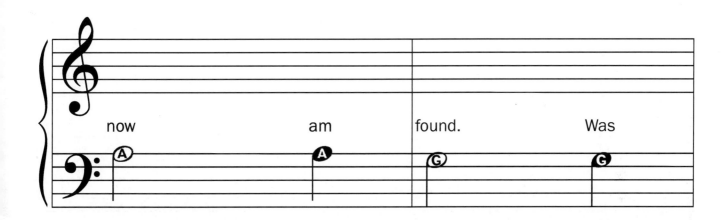

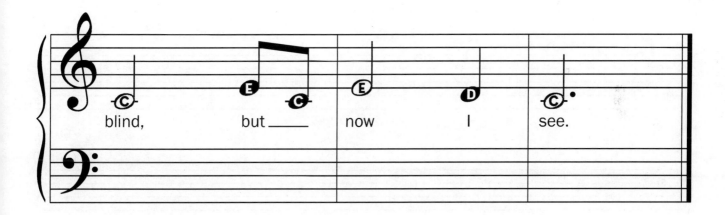

William Tell Overture

Thumbs Are Neighbors Position

Gioachino Rossini

Oh My Darling, Clementine

Thumbs Are Neighbors Position

Percy Montrose

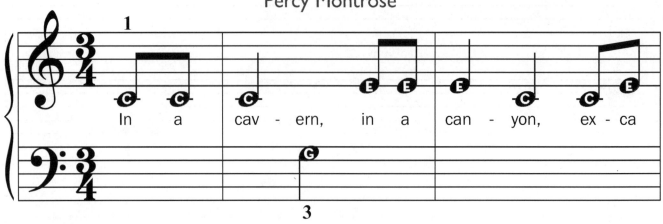

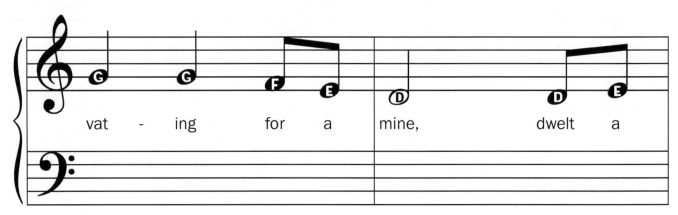

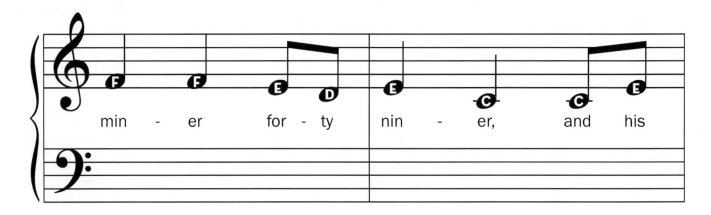

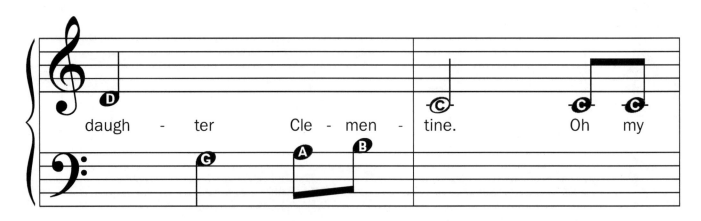

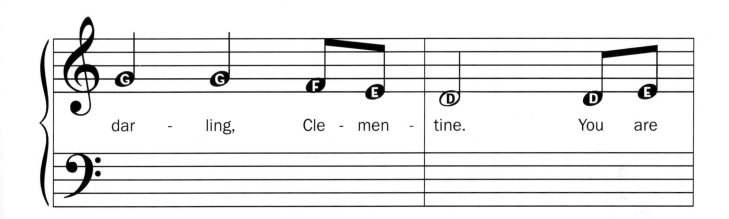

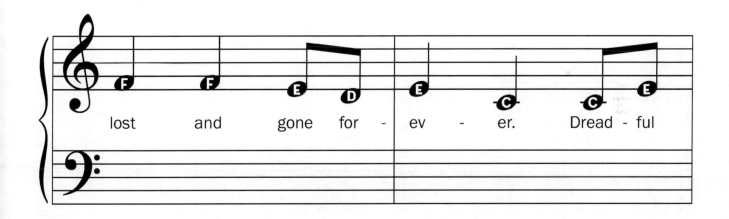

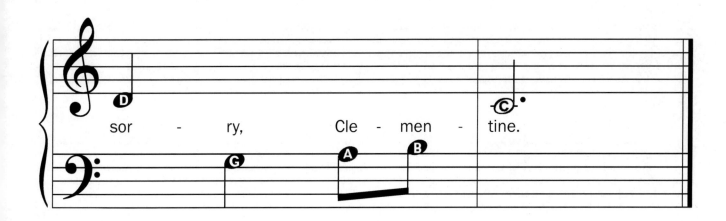

Für Elise

Thumbs Are Neighbors Position
Ludwig van Beethoven

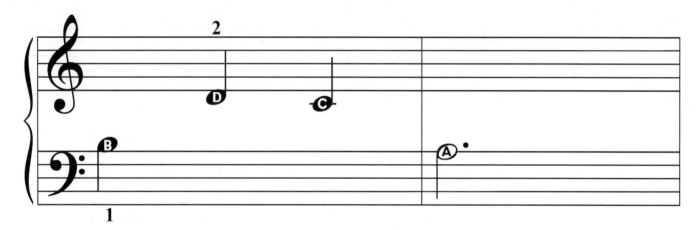

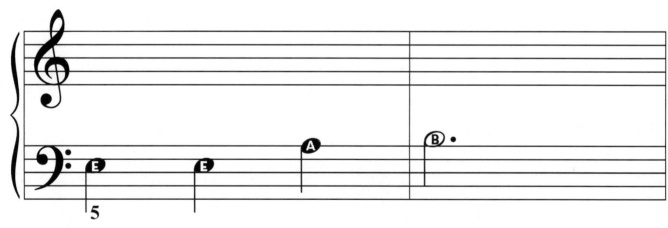

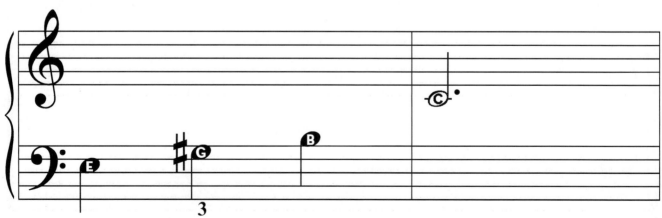

The House of the Rising Sun

Thumbs Are Neighbors Position

American Folk Song

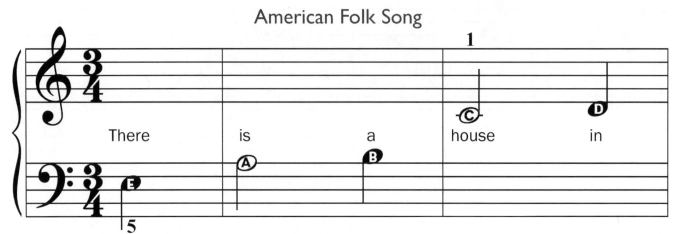

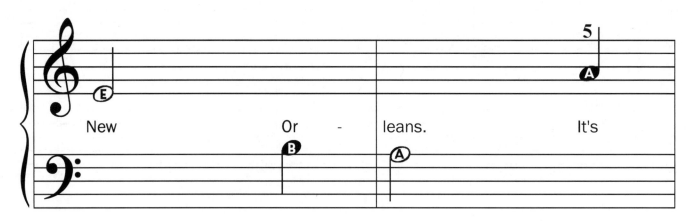

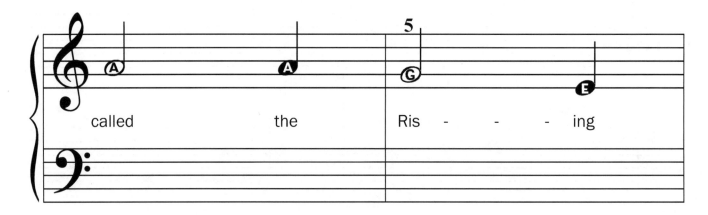

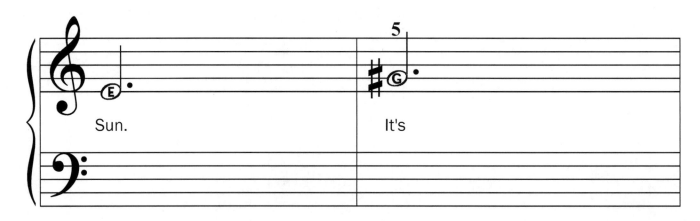

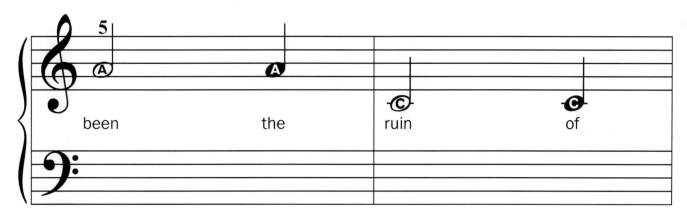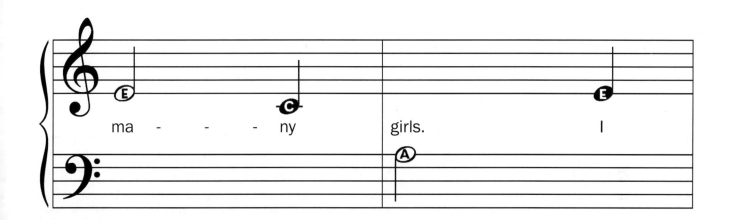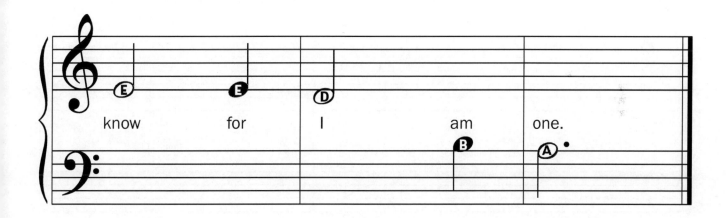

John Jacob Jingleheimer Schmidt

Thumbs Are Neighbors Position
Traditional Children's Song

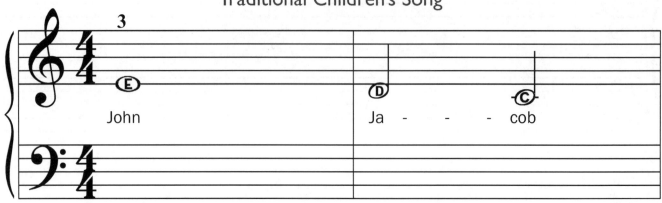

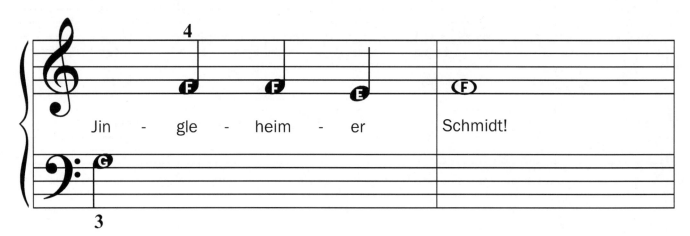

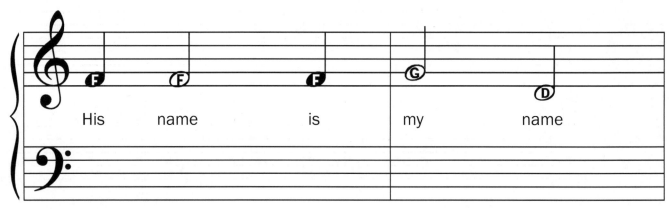

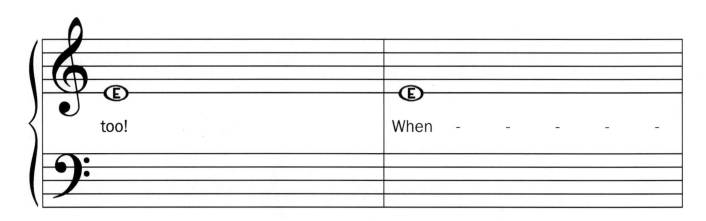

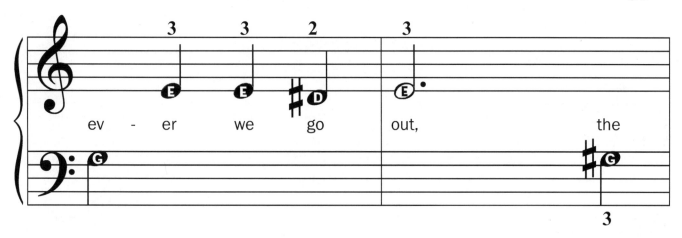

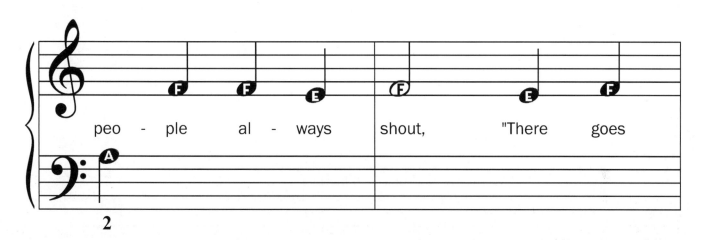

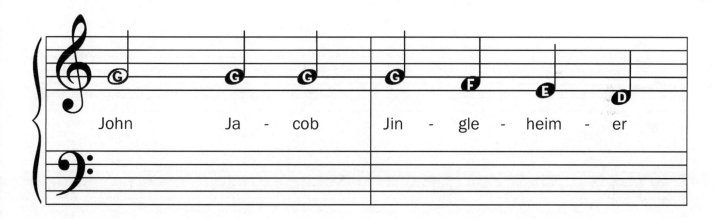

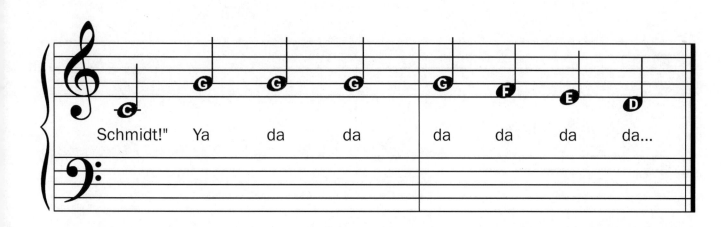

My Country 'Tis of Thee

Thumbs Are Neighbors Position

Samuel Francis Smith

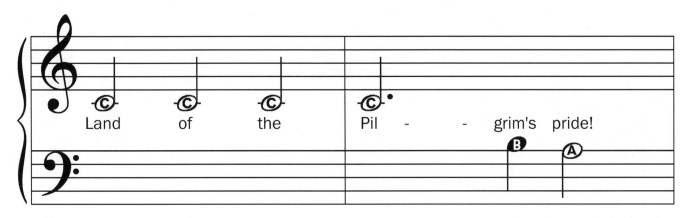

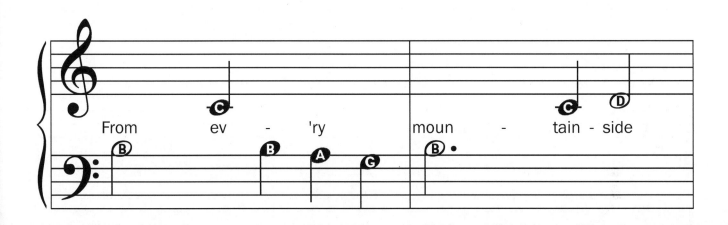

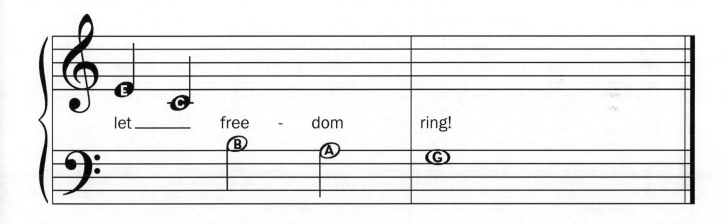

Take Me Out to the Ballgame

Thumbs are Neighbors Position

Albert Von Tilzer and Jack Norworth

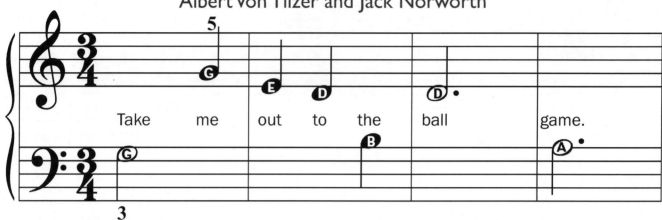

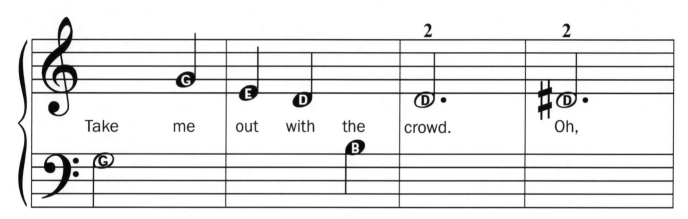

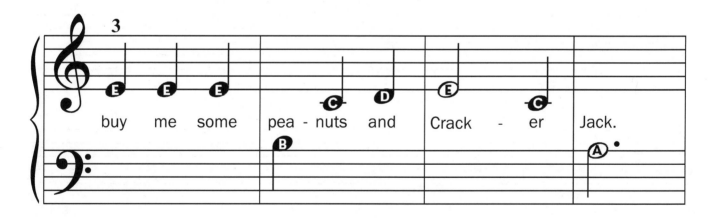

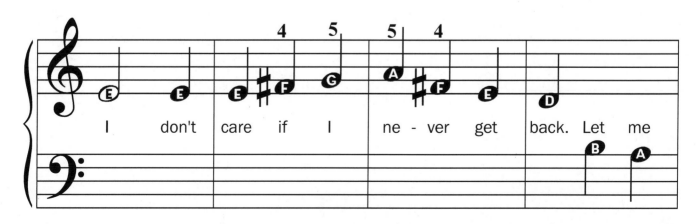

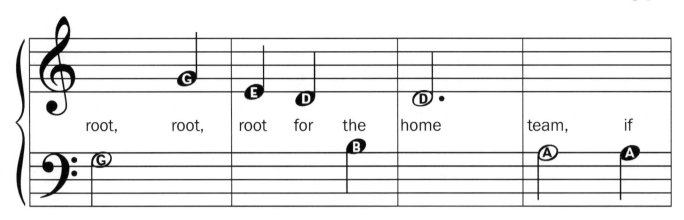

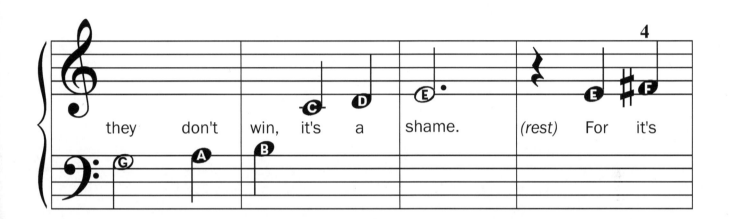

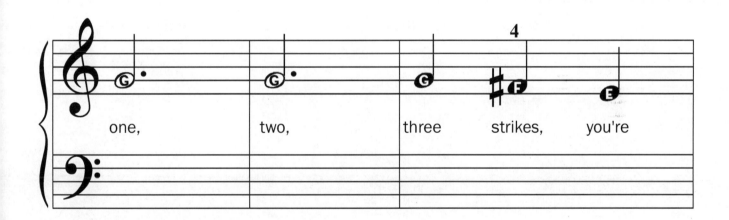

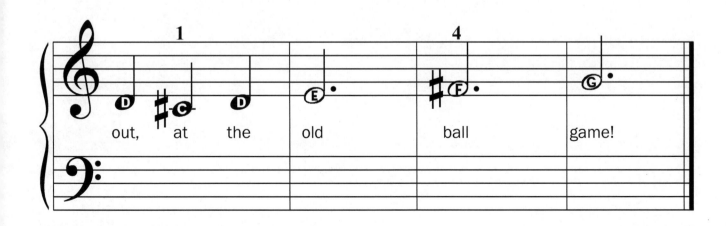

C Scale: Easy

All Songs in This Section Use
C Scale Position

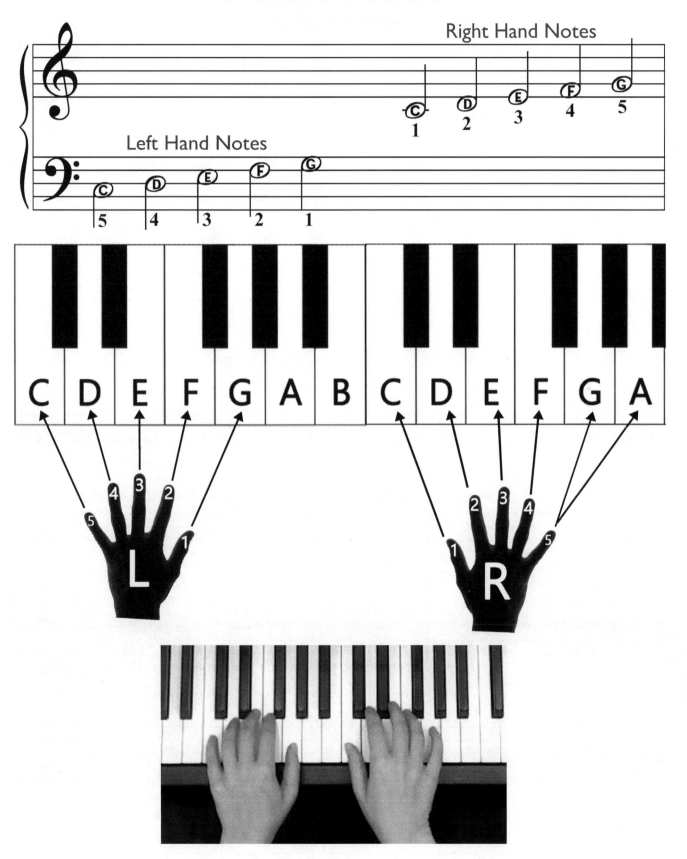

Practice placing your hands in this position until you can do it quickly and easily.

Left Hand Solo

C Scale Position

Angela Marshall

C Scale Steps

C Scale Position

Angela Marshall

Itsy Bitsy Spider

C Scale Position

American Folk Song

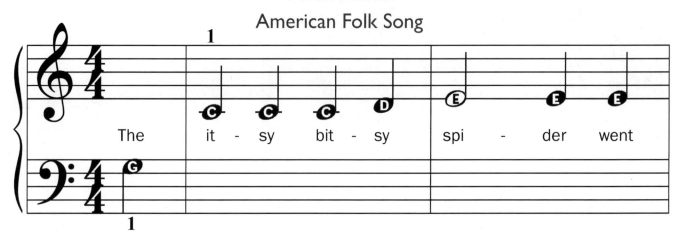

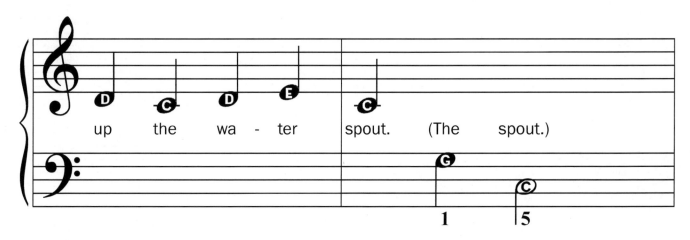

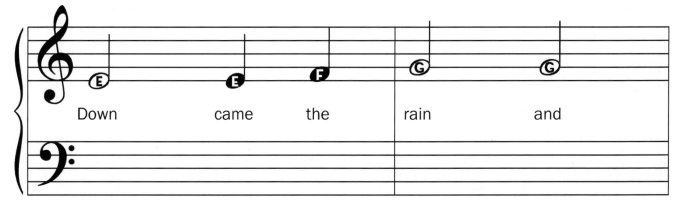

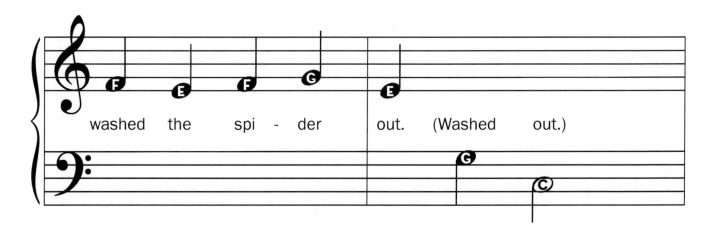

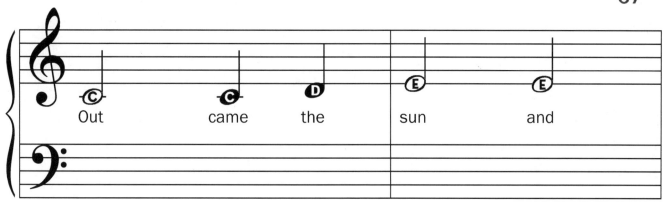

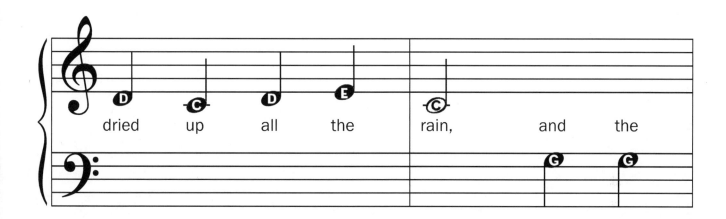

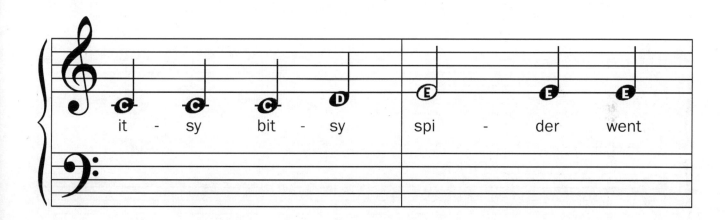

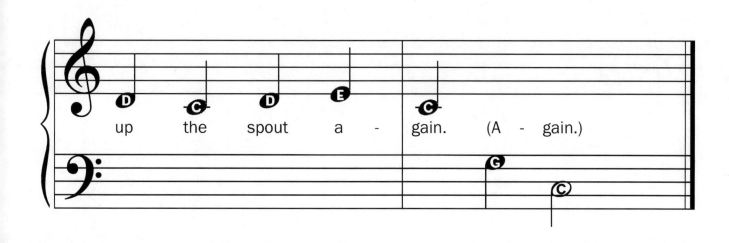

Row, Row, Row Your Boat

C Scale Position

Folk Song

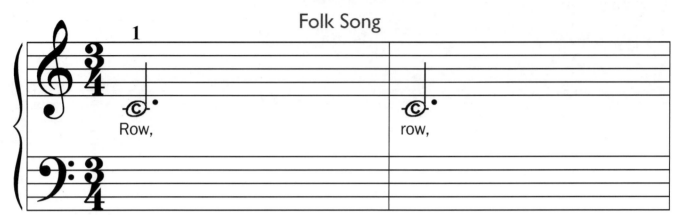

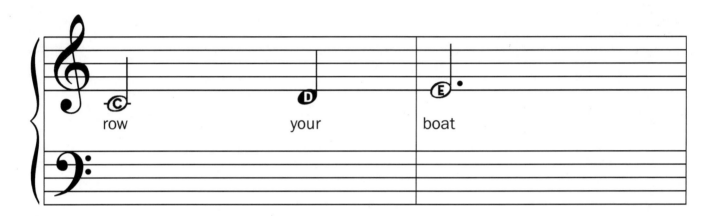

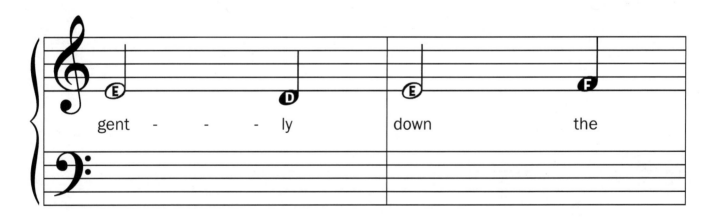

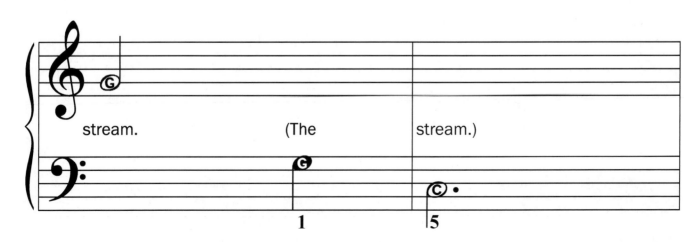

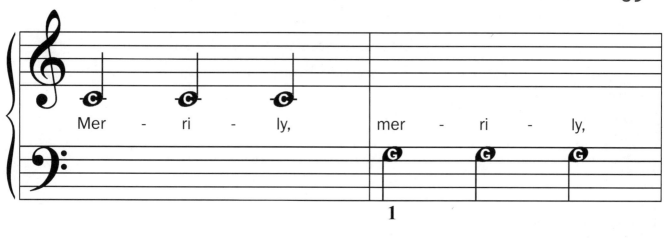

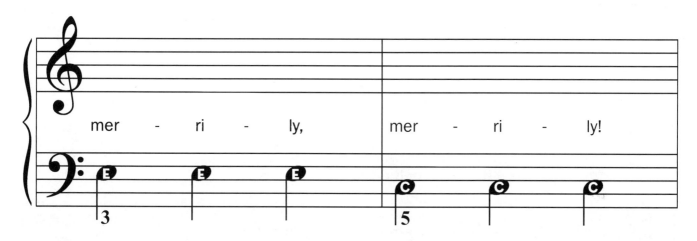

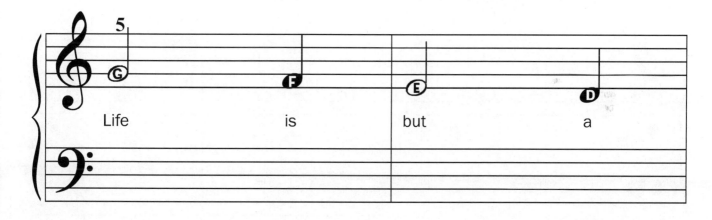

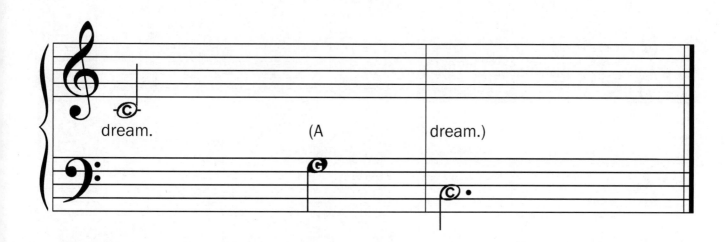

The Farmer in the Dell

C Scale Position

German Folk Song

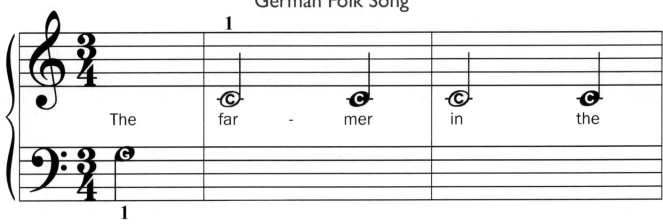

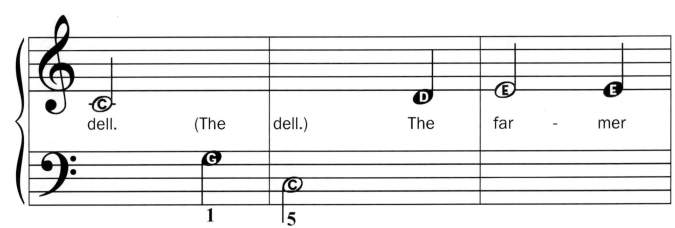

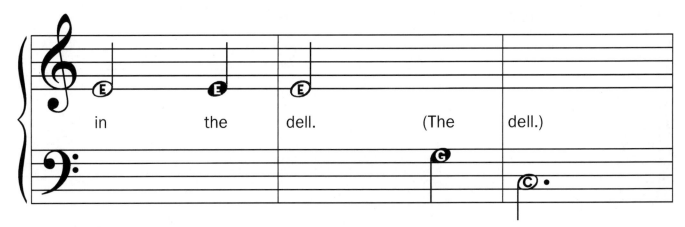

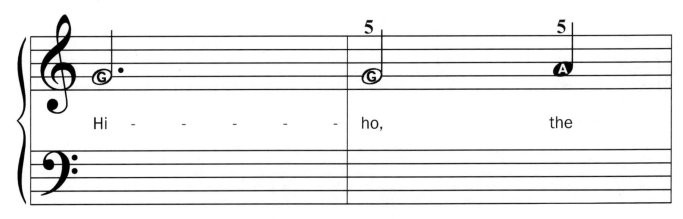

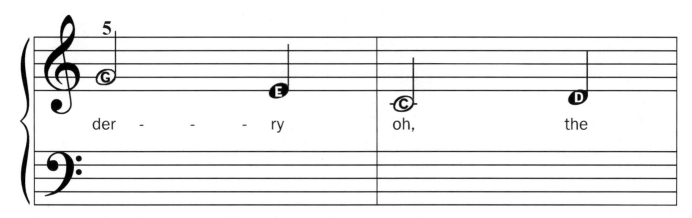

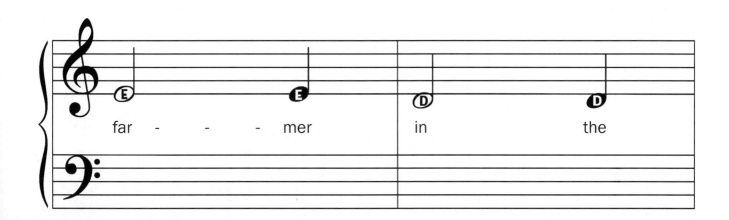

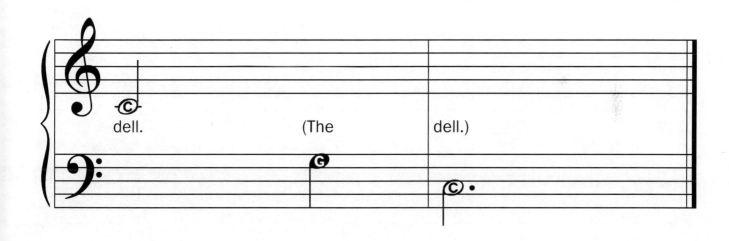

Rondeau

C Scale Position

Jean-Joseph Mouret

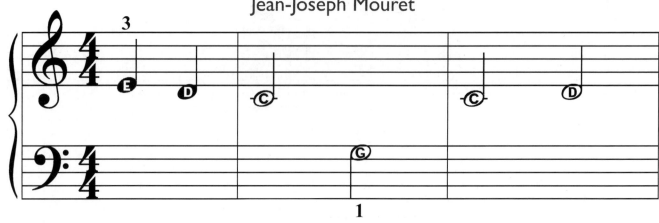

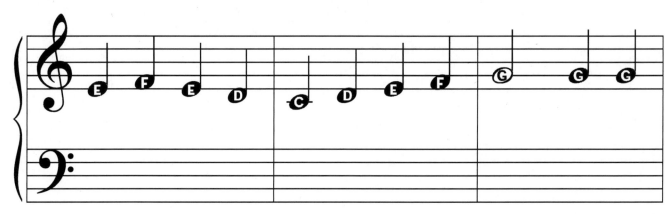

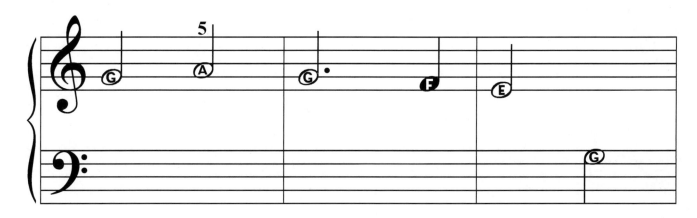

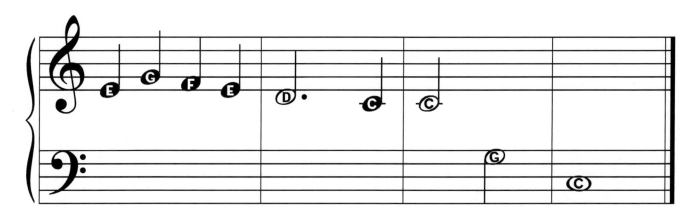

Al Citrón

C Scale Position

Mexican Folk Song

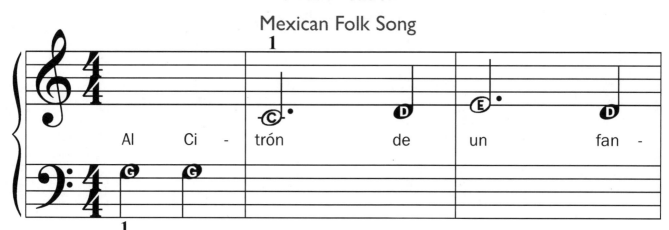

Al Ci - trón de un fan -

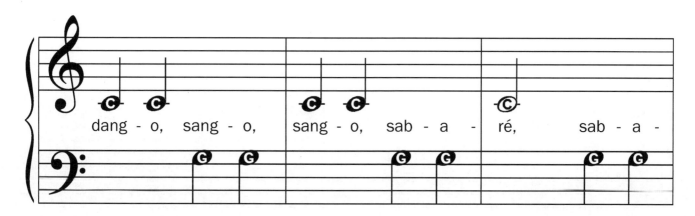

dang - o, sang - o, sang - o, sab - a - ré, sab - a -

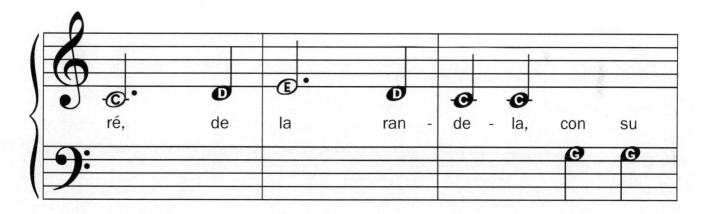

ré, de la ran - de - la, con su

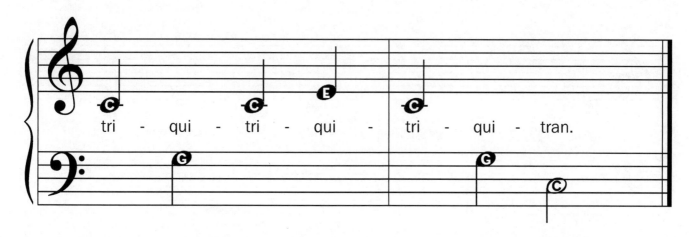

tri - qui - tri - qui - tri - qui tran.

Mama Don't 'Low

C Scale Position

American Folk Song

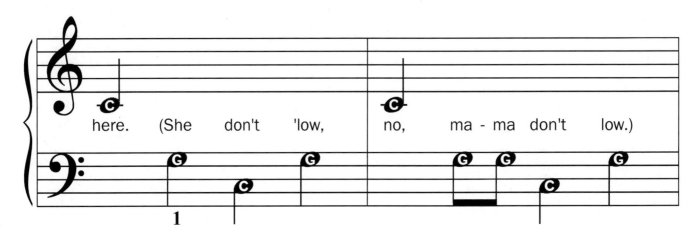

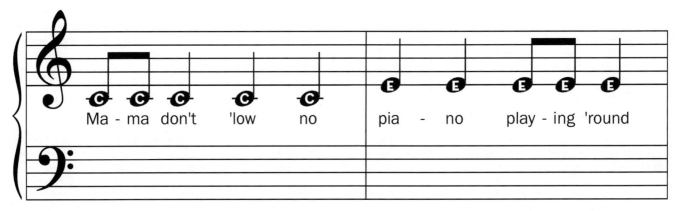

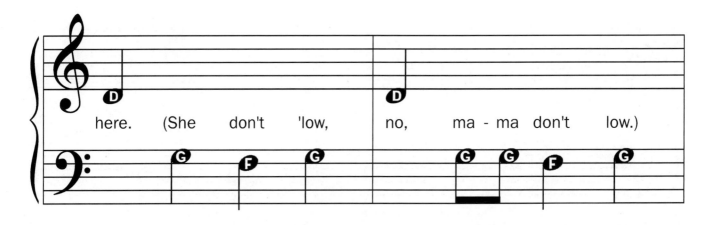

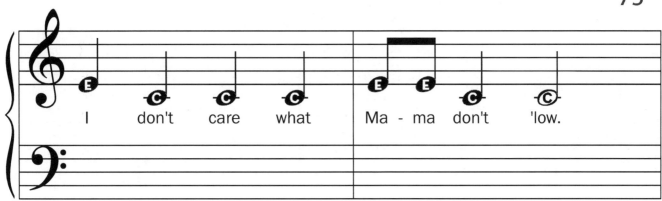

I don't care what Ma - ma don't 'low.

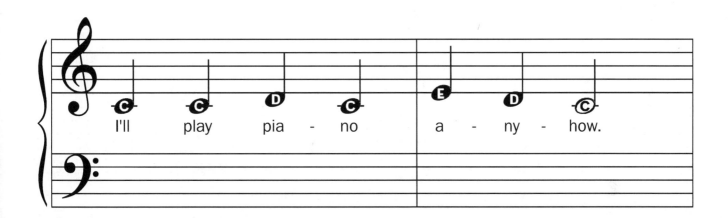

I'll play pia - no a - ny - how.

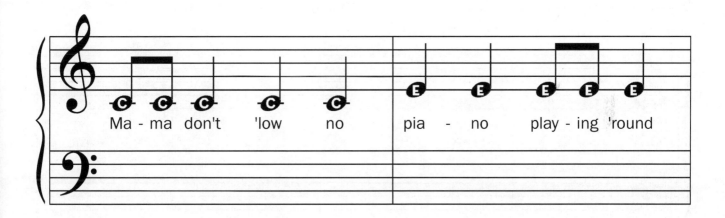

Ma - ma don't 'low no pia - no play - ing 'round

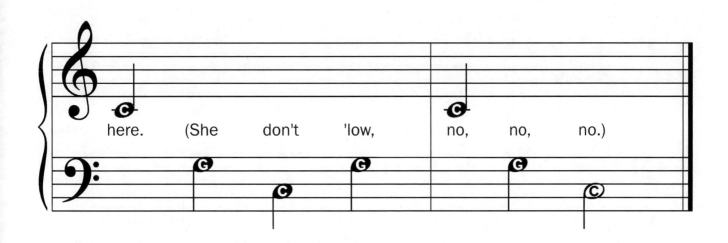

here. (She don't 'low, no, no, no.)

Alouette

C Scale Position

French-Canadian Folk Song

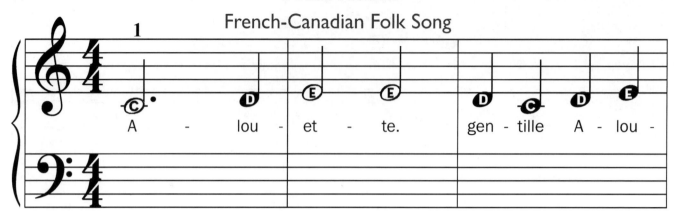

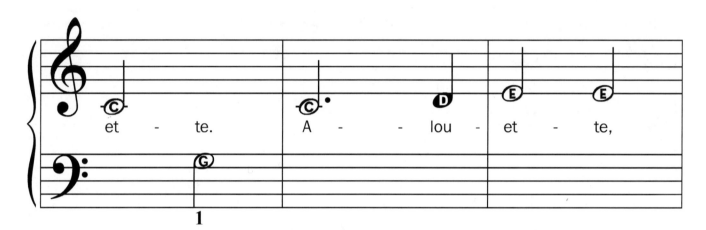

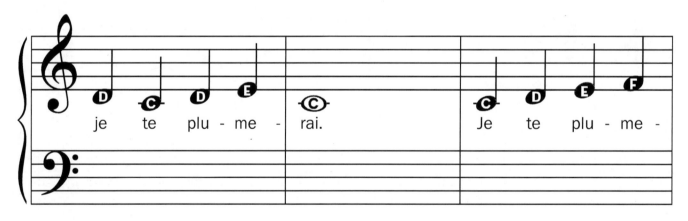

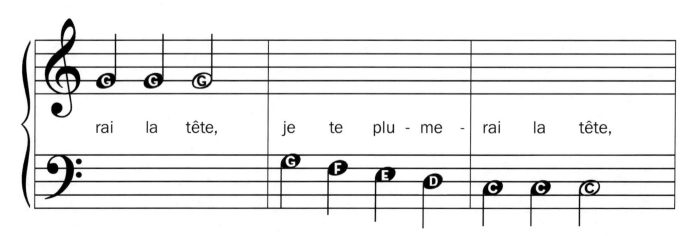

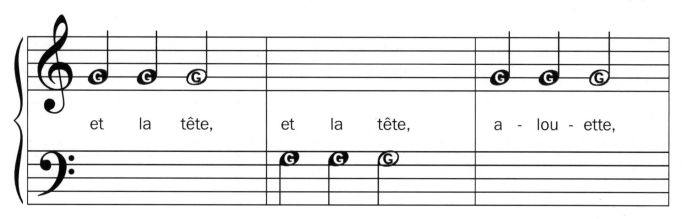

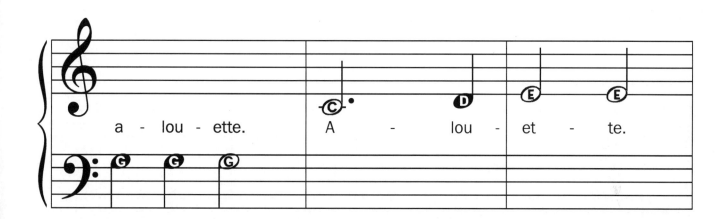

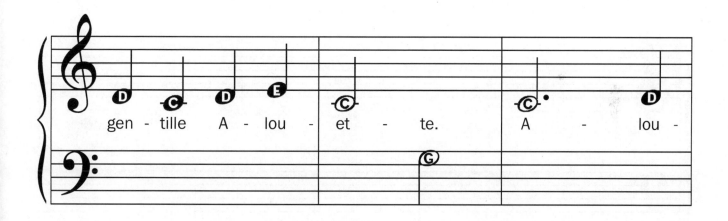

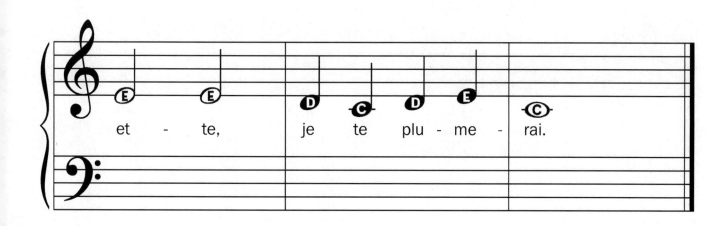

Hornpipe from Water Music

C Scale Position

George Frideric Handel

C Scale: Challenge

All Songs in This Section Use C Scale Position
But you will play multiple notes at the same time!

Notes that align vertically
will be played together.

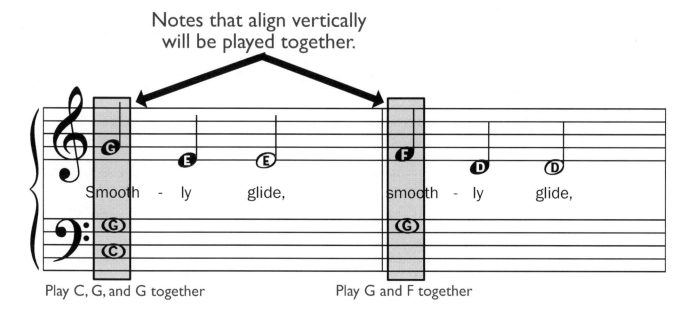

Play C, G, and G together   Play G and F together

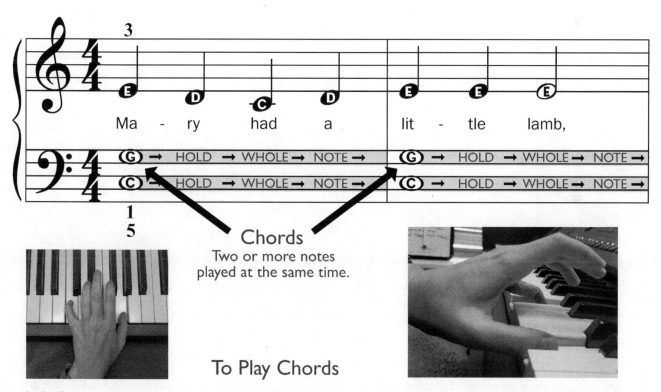

Chords
Two or more notes
played at the same time.

To Play Chords

Lift fingers 2, 3, 4 slightly and lower your arm to play fingers 5 and 1 together.

Technique Tip
To play notes with both hands at the same time, slightly lift the fingers that are not playing, then lower both arms at the same time. It is easier to coordinate your arms than individual fingers.

Two Notes

C Scale Position

Angela Marshall

Playing Chords

C Scale Position

Angela Marshall

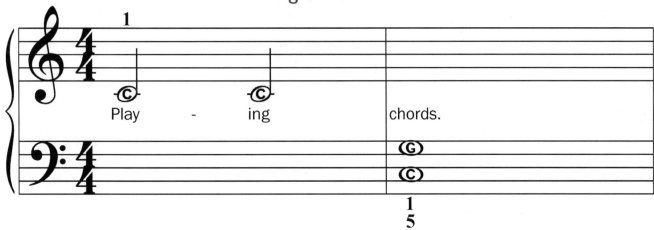

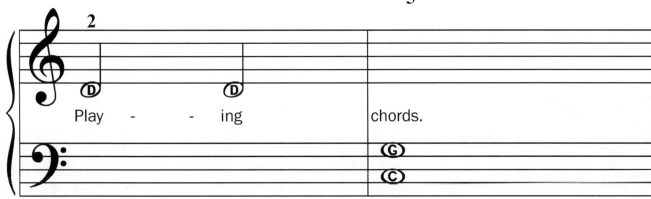

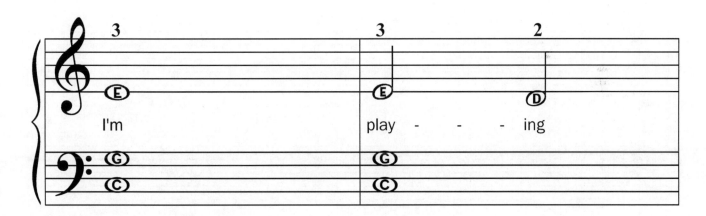

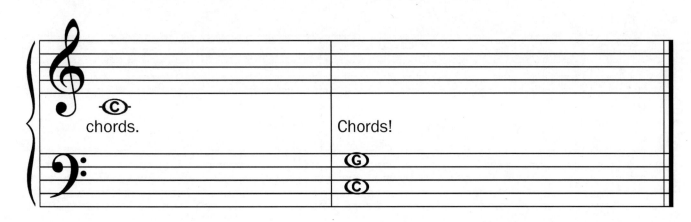

84

Sally Go 'Round the Sun

C Scale Position

Folk Song

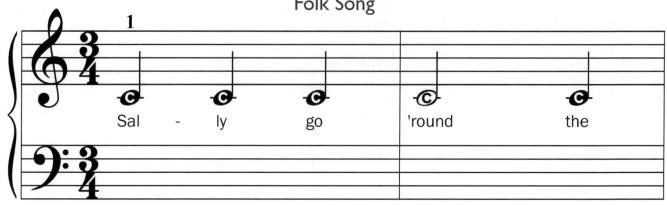

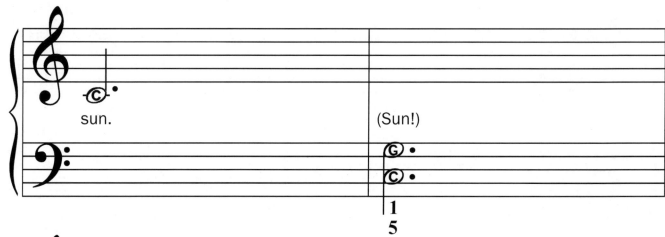

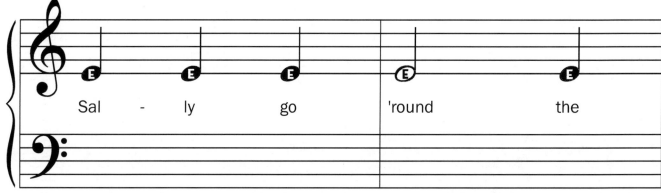

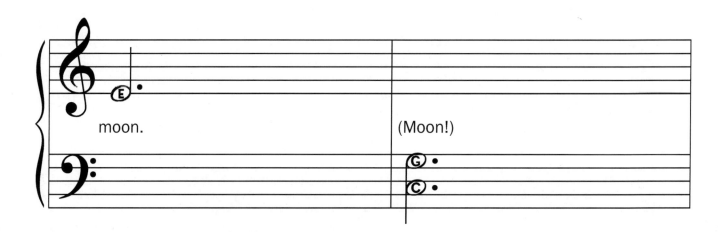

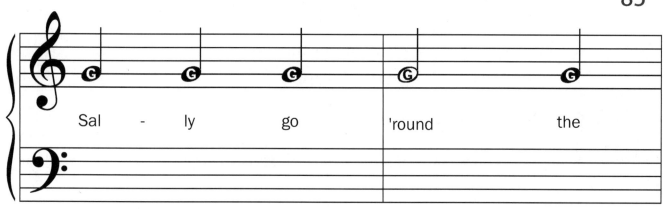

Sal - ly go 'round the

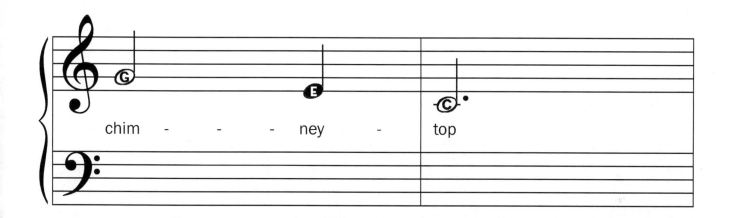

chim - - - ney - top

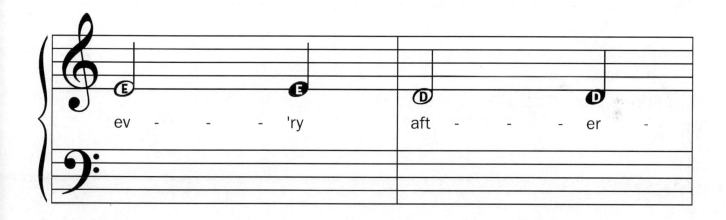

ev - - - 'ry aft - - - er -

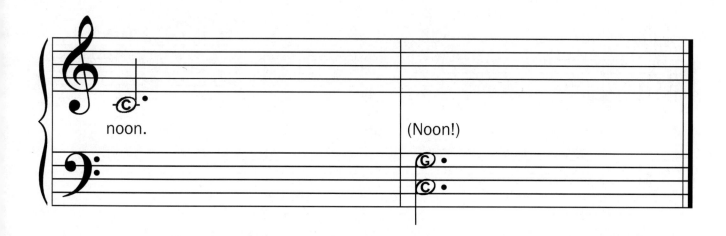

noon. (Noon!)

Jingle Bells

C Scale Position

James Pierpont

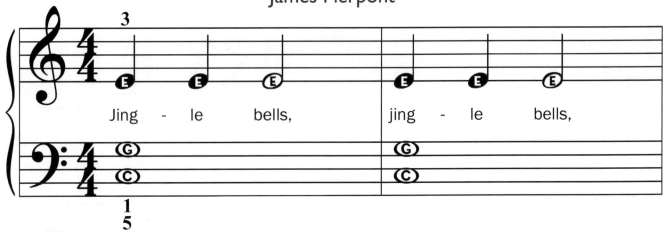

Jing - le bells, jing - le bells,

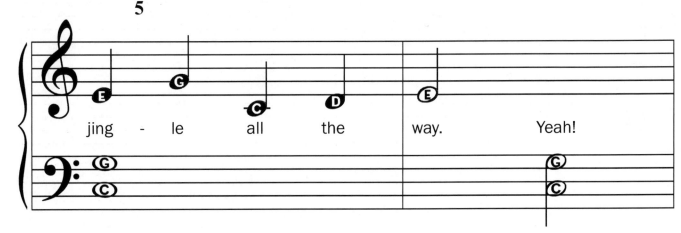

jing - le all the way. Yeah!

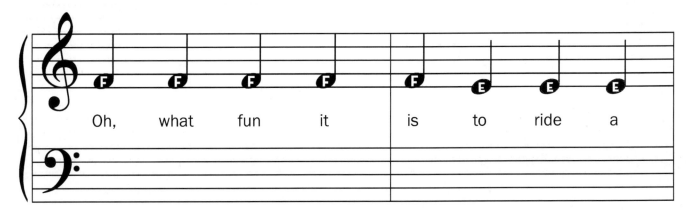

Oh, what fun it is to ride a

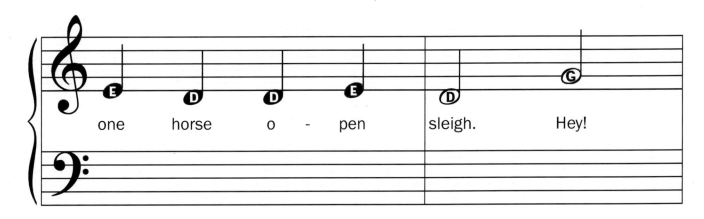

one horse o - pen sleigh. Hey!

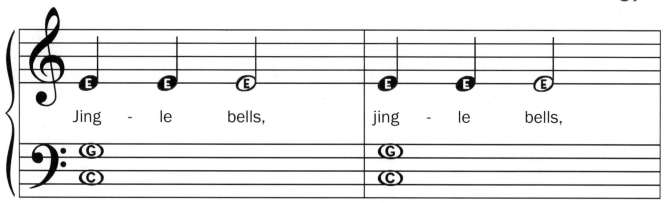

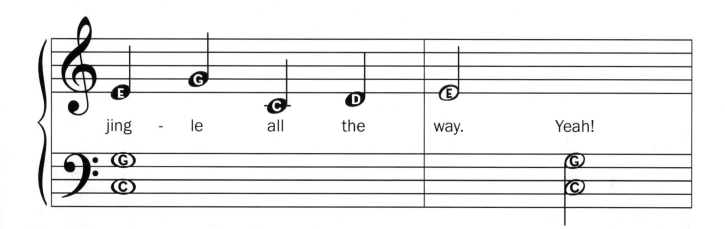

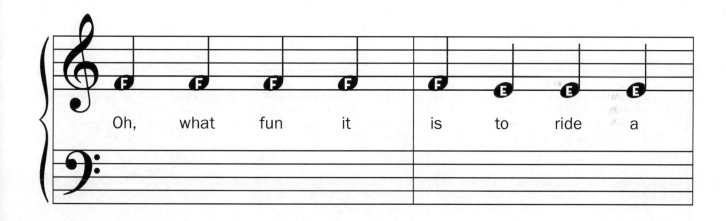

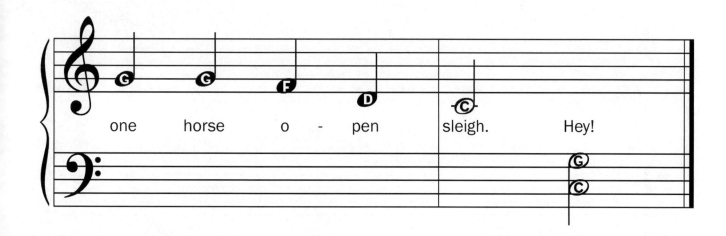

Hot Cross Buns

C Scale Position

English Folk Song

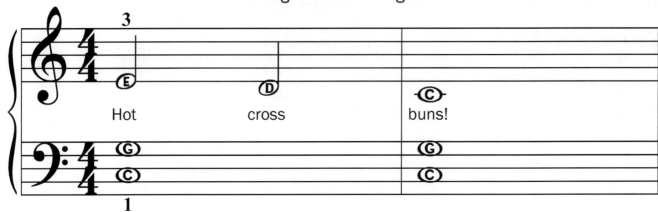

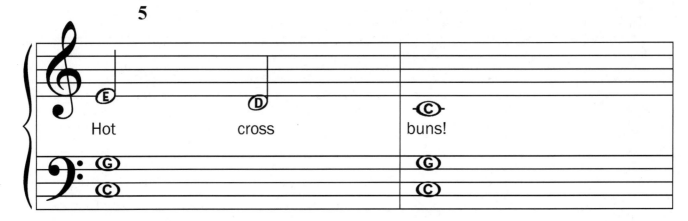

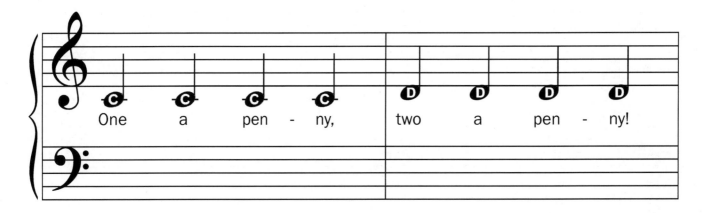

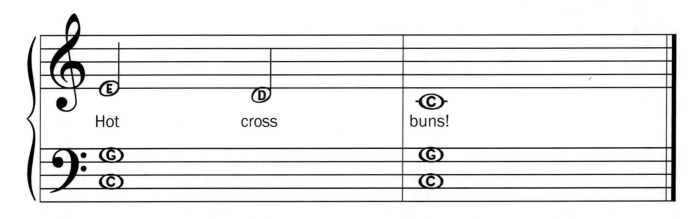

Au Clair de la Lune

C Scale Position

French Folk Song

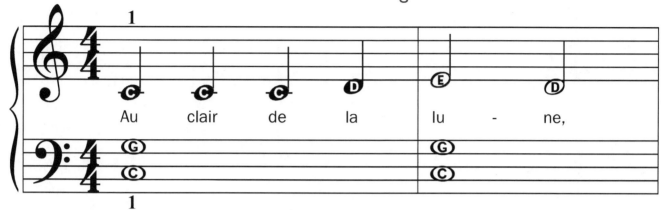

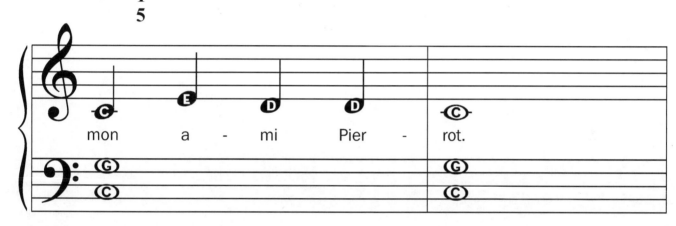

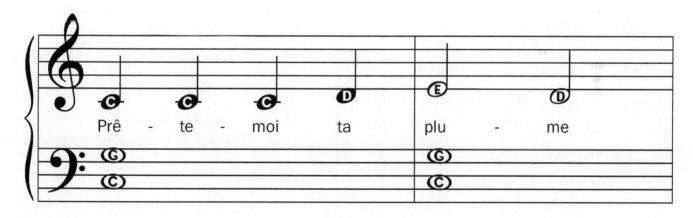

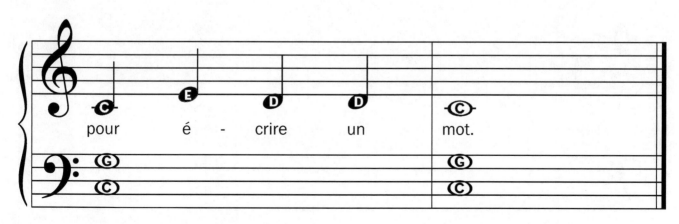

Mary Had a Little Lamb

C Scale Position

American Folk Song

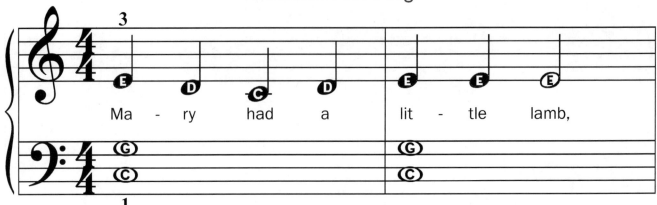

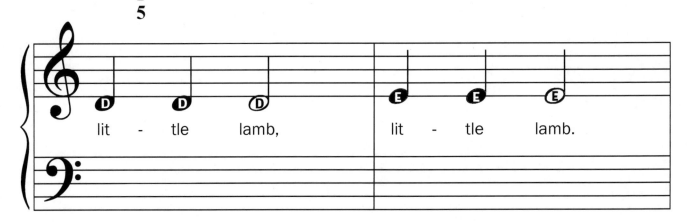

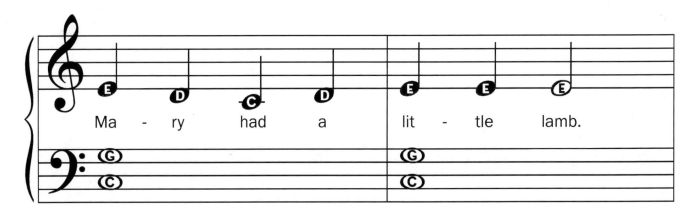

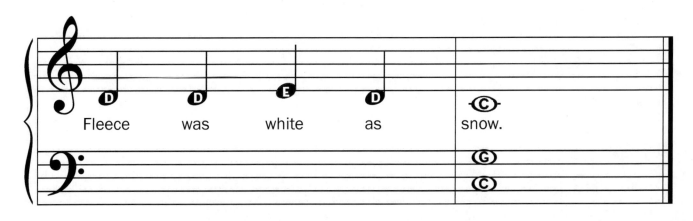

Largo from New World Symphony

C Scale Position

Antonín Dvořák

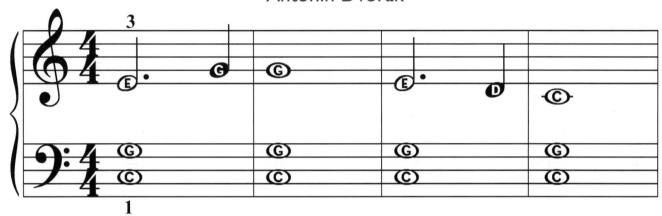

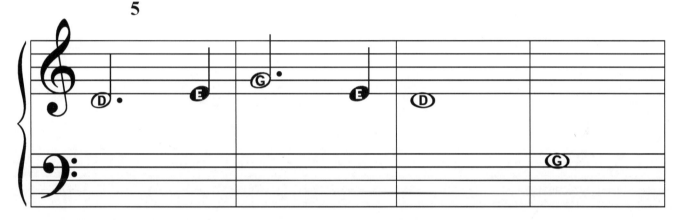

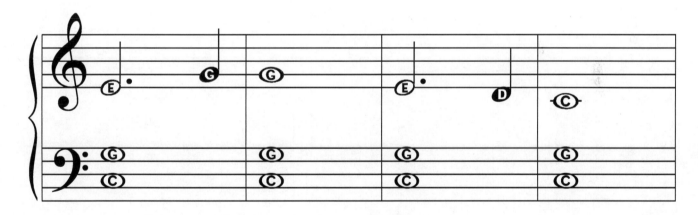

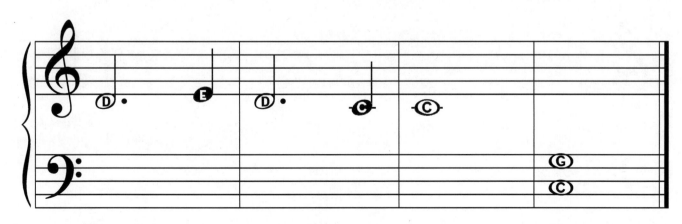

Sweetly Sings the Donkey

C Scale Position

Folk Song

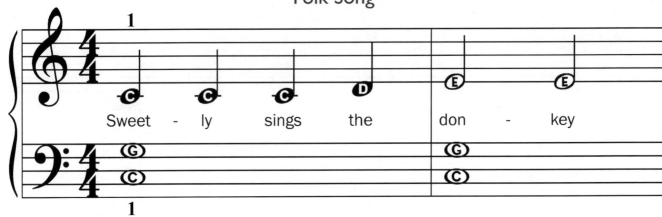

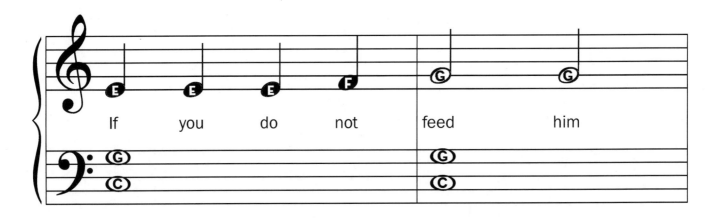

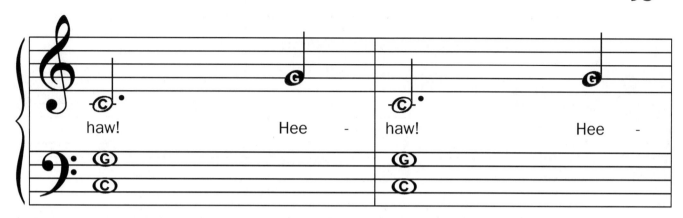

haw!   Hee -   haw!   Hee -

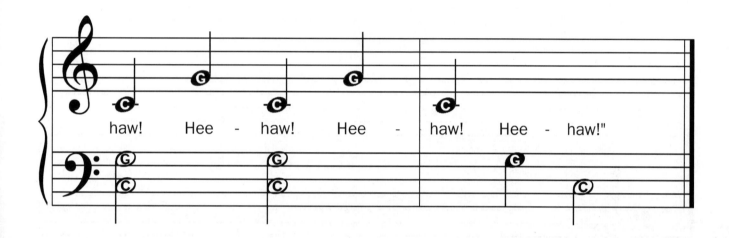

haw!   Hee - haw!   Hee - haw!   Hee - haw!"

Are You Sleeping

C Scale Position

French Folk Song

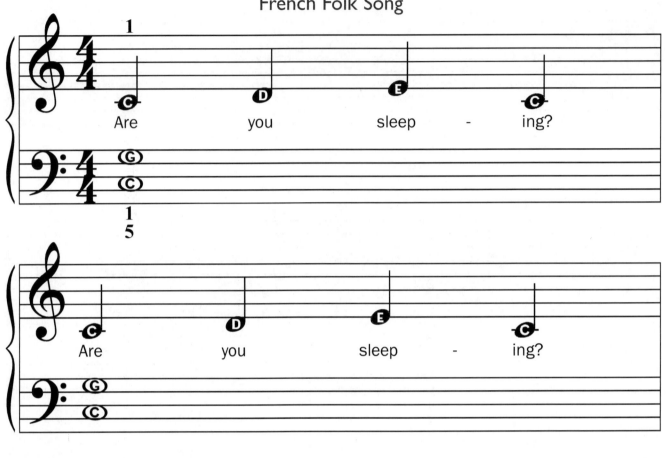

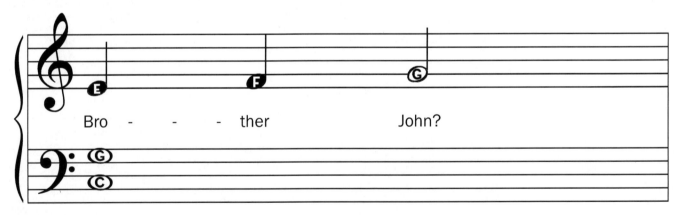

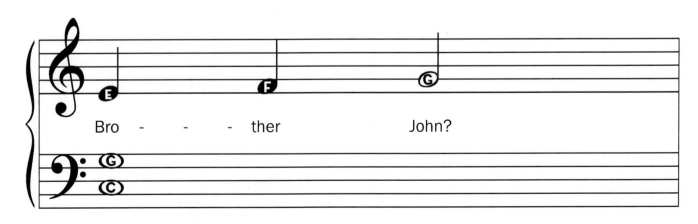

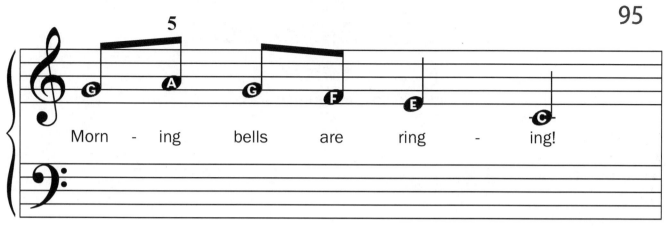

Morn - ing bells are ring - ing!

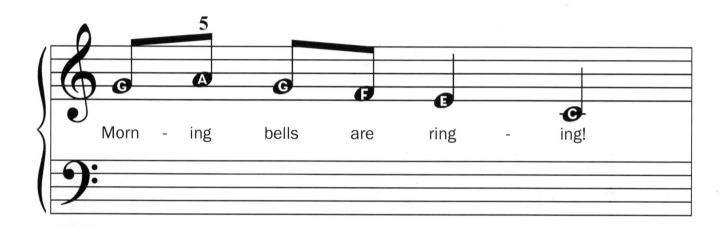

Morn - ing bells are ring - ing!

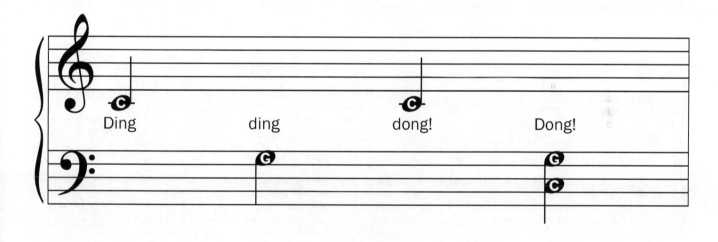

Ding ding dong! Dong!

Ding ding dong! Dong!

The Dreidel Song

C Scale Position

Traditional Hanukkah Song

Oh, drei - del, drei - del, drei - del! I

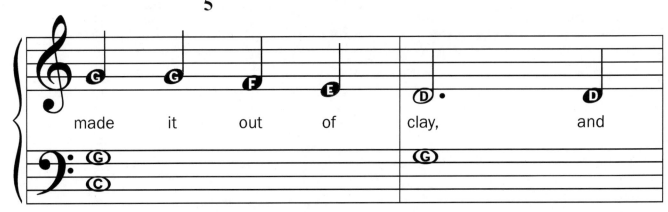

made it out of clay, and

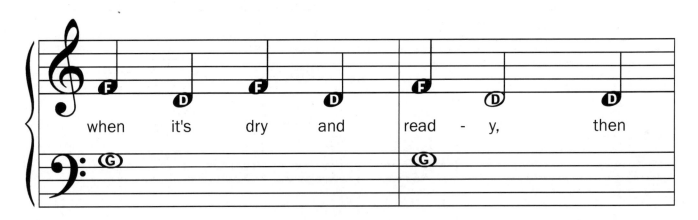

when it's dry and read - y, then

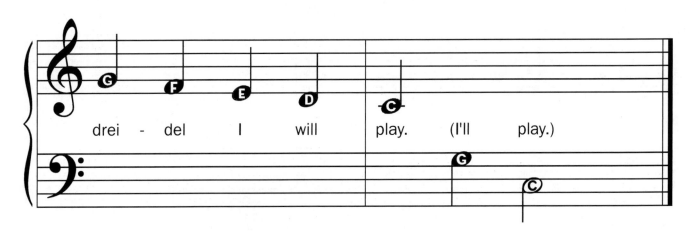

drei - del I will play. (I'll play.)

Go Tell Aunt Rhody

C Scale Position

American Folk Song

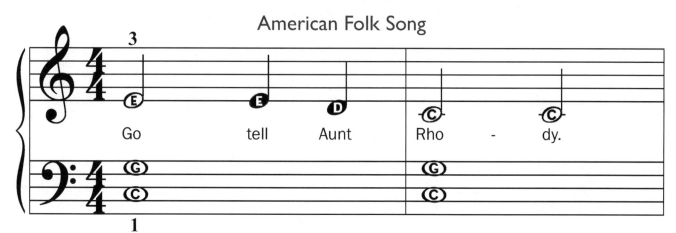

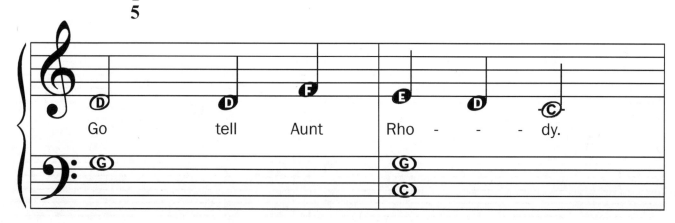

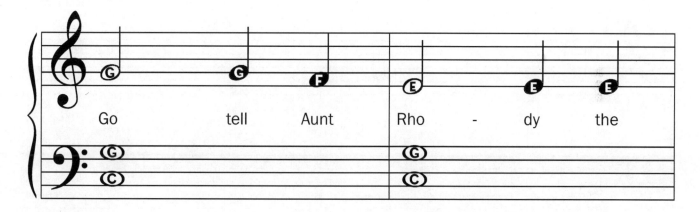

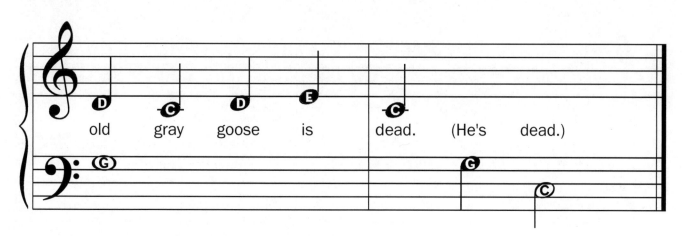

Ode to Joy

C Scale Position

Ludwig van Beethoven

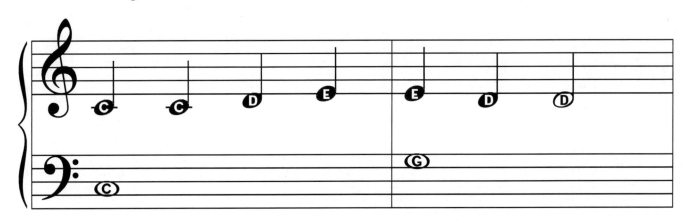

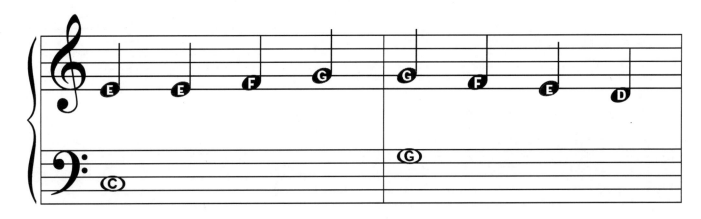

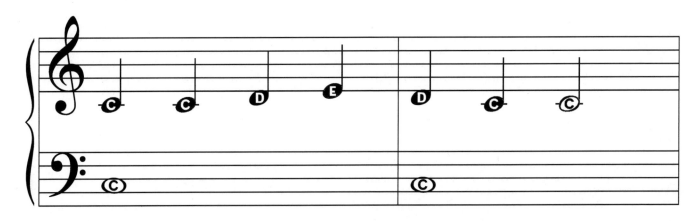

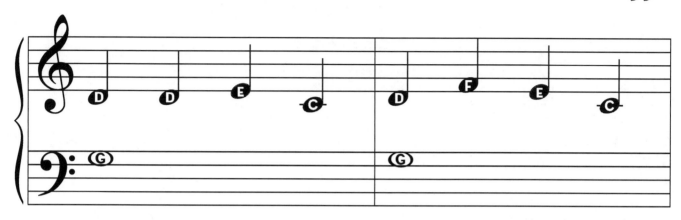

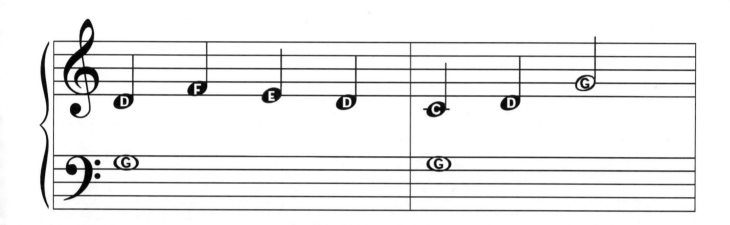

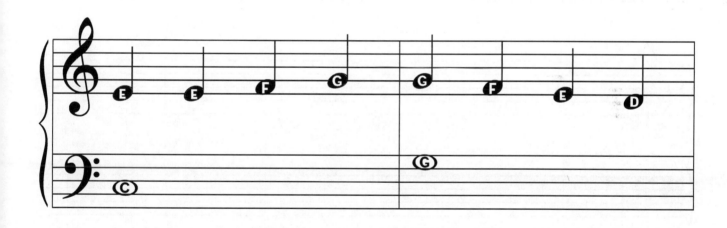

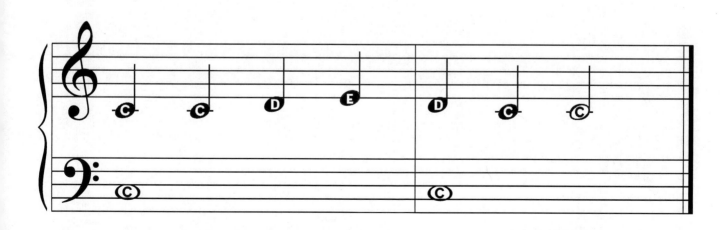

Hush, Little Baby

C Scale Position

American Folk Song

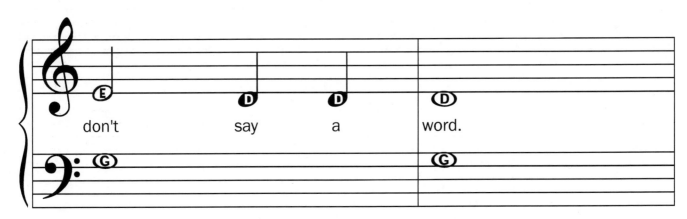

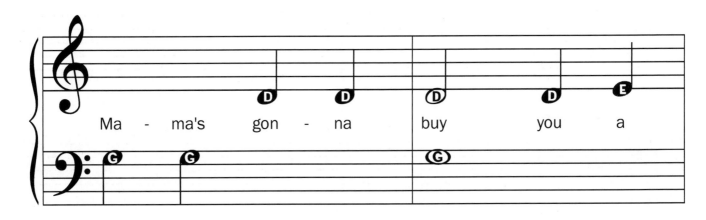

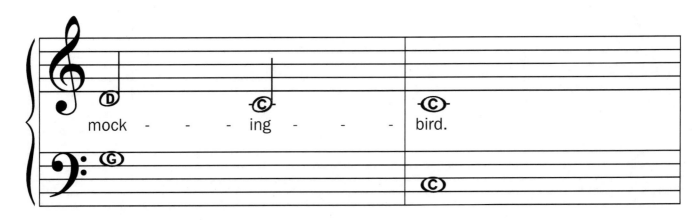

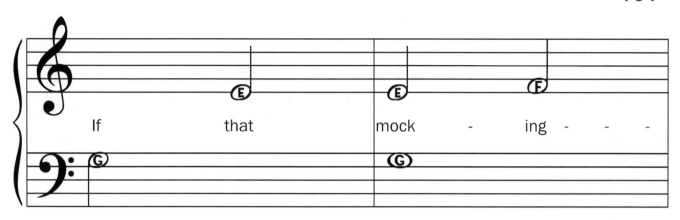

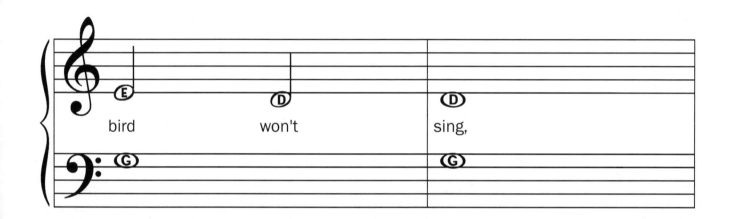

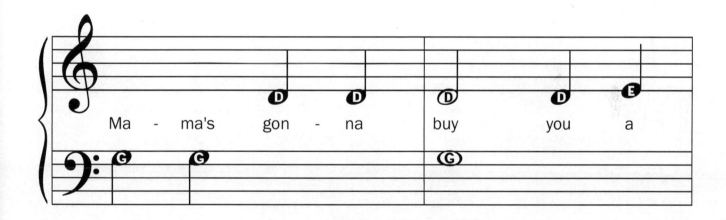

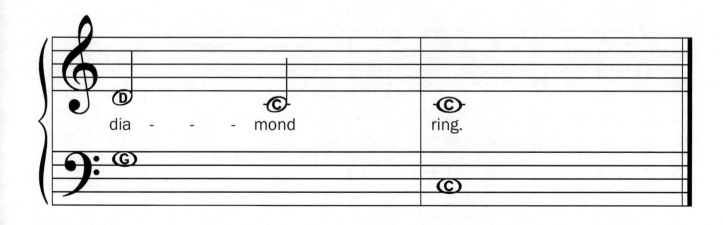

102

Lightly Row

C Scale Position

American Folk Song from German Melody

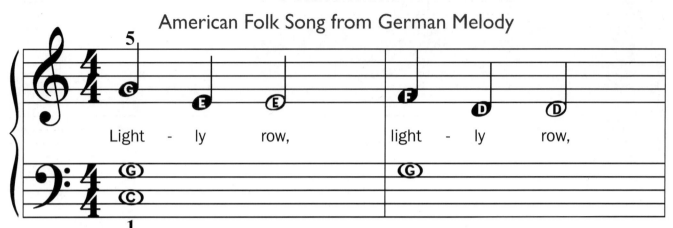

Light - ly row, light - ly row,

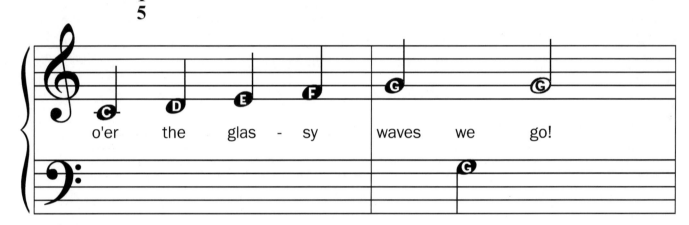

o'er the glas - sy waves we go!

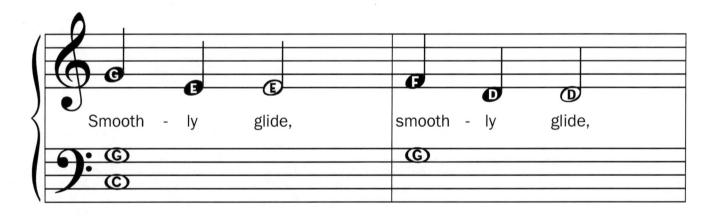

Smooth - ly glide, smooth - ly glide,

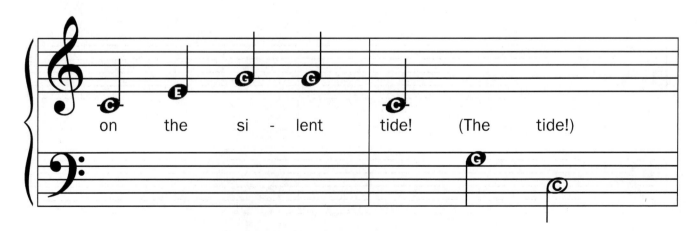

on the si - lent tide! (The tide!)

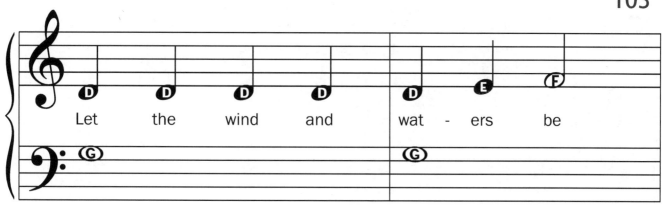

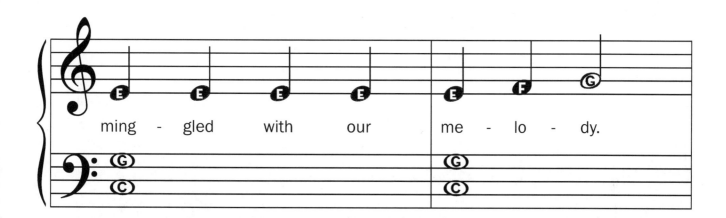

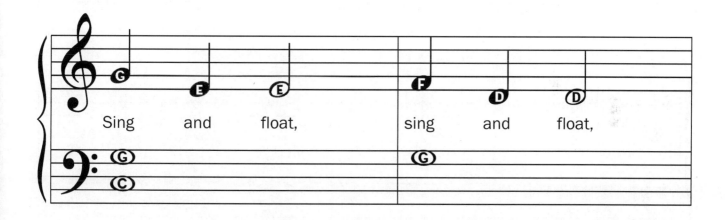

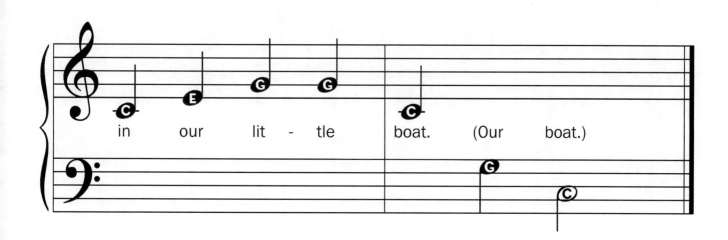

Pop! Goes the Weasel

C Scale Position

English Folk Song

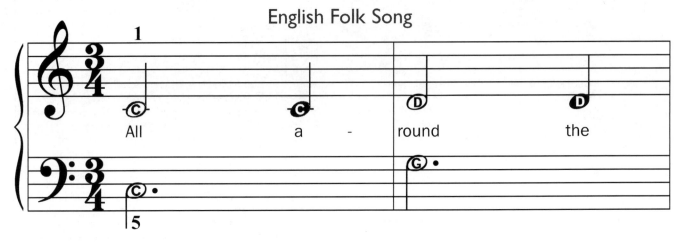

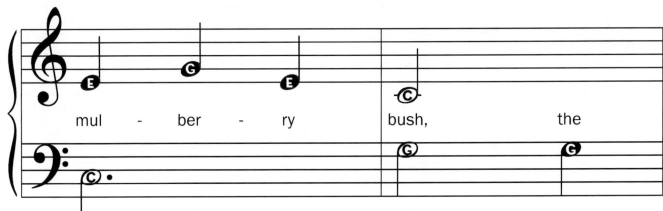

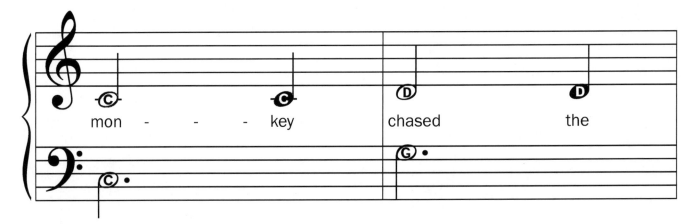

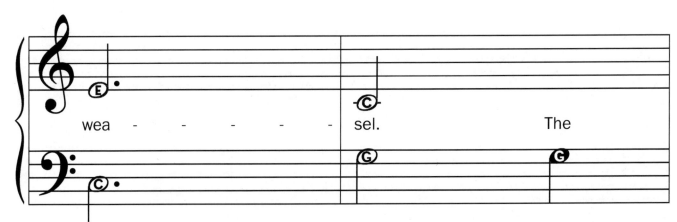

When the Saints Go Marching In

C Scale Position

African American Spiritual

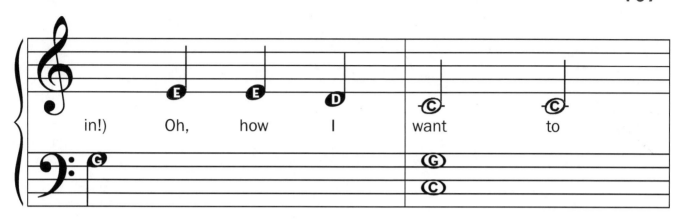

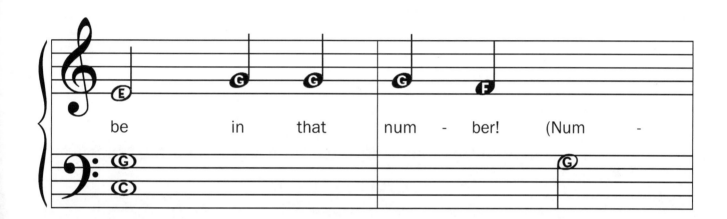

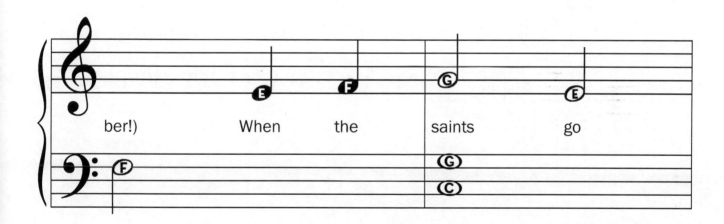

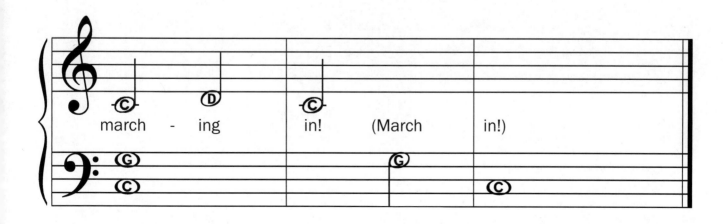

Bonus Downloads

This book includes free digital content.
Visit **www.avanellpublishing.com** or scan the QR code below
to access your bonus materials,

- Fully orchestrated recordings of each song

- Printable reference charts to use while you play

Made in United States
Troutdale, OR
02/01/2025

28568331R00062